The Kids' Book of
WeaTher
ForecasTing

Build a weather station, "read" the sky & make predictions!

With meteorologist Mark Breen & Kathleen Friestad

williamsonbooks™

Nashville, Tennessee

ISBN-13: 978-0-8249-6823-6 (softcover)
ISBN-13: 978-0-8249-6822-9 (hardcover)

Published by Williamson Books
An imprint of Ideals Publications, a Guideposts Company
Nashville, Tennessee
www.idealsbooks.com

Printed and bound in China

Library of Congress Cataloging-in-Publication Data
Breen, Mark, 1960–
    The kids' book of weather forecasting : build a weather station, "read" the sky & make predictions
with meteorologist Mark Breen and Kathleen Friestad; illustrations by Michael Kline.
        p. cm.
    A Williamson kids can! book.
    Includes index.
    Summary: A hands-on introduction to the science of meteorology, explaining how to make
equipment to measure rainfall, wind direction, and humidity, record measurements and observations
in a weather log, make weather predictions, and perform other related activities.
    1. Weather forecasting—Juvenile literature. [1. Weather—Experiments. 2. Meteorology—Experiments.
3. Weather forecasting. 4. Experiments.] I. Friestad, Kathleen, 1968– II. Kline, Michael P., ill. III. Title.
QC981.3 .B723 2000
551.63—dc21   99-089954

Kids Can!® Series Editor: Susan Williamson
Project Editor: Vicky Congdon
Designed by: Marisa Jackson

Kids Can!® is a registered trademark of Ideals Publications.

Reg_Sept14_4

**To my three children—Sean, Meghan, and Rose—for the magic of seeing the
    world anew through their eyes. —Mark Breen**
To my husband, Greg, who always reminds me that science can be fun! —Kathleen Friestad

ACKNOWLEDGMENTS: Thanks to the Fairbanks Museum and Planetarium in St. Johnsbury, Vermont; to William Cotte for deciphering the music for "The Weatherman Song"; to the many people who have shared their weather stories with me; to Mom and Dad for that first barometer; and to my dearest Carol. —Mark Breen

    Mark, your enthusiasm for all aspects of the weather is contagious! It has been a pleasure to work with you! Peter and Kim Landry have been mentors—the first to encourage me to write for the next generation. Susan Williamson envisioned this book and gave it life, and throughout its creation, Vicky Congdon shaped and nurtured it with editorial expertise, professionalism, and commitment. My sincere thanks to all of you! —Kathleen Friestad

PERMISSIONS: Permission to use the following material is granted by Ideals Publications: page 55, Tales of the Shimmering Sky by Susan Milord. Photographs on pages 107, 110, 113, and 128 are used by permission of the National Oceanic and Atmospheric Administration/Department of Commerce. Weather map on page 116 is courtesy of USA Today.

Contents

WHY DID I BECOME A METEOROLOGIST?

Plain and simple—because I love snow! That's right! It was two storms in particular that got me excited about understanding the weather. When I was nine years old, a huge snowstorm buried the northeastern United States. The wind blew a drift in my backyard that was four feet (1.2 m) high and 20 feet (6 m) long! My brothers and sisters and I spent days tunneling through that snow. It was great!

Nine years later (after I had already decided to be a meteorologist), there was another huge storm that turned into a blizzard. I remember tracking the storm and measuring the wind and the snowfall. I also remember waking up the next morning and seeing two giant white lumps in the driveway. Those lumps were our cars under 40 inches (1 m) of snow! It meant a lot of shoveling, to be sure; but I still was excited by all that snow.

When I started forecasting more than 20 years ago, computers were a new technology found in only the most sophisticated weather offices. I would draw weather maps by hand and color-code them. I used to laugh that I had the only job that would pay me to color! Of course, a great deal has changed since then—but there are still times when I color parts of the weather map. I can only imagine what this new century will bring for us forecasters. But one thing I am certain of, there will be plenty of weather!

Once you begin exploring the four main components of weather—air, sun, wind, and water—you'll see that it's not such a mystery after all. You'll create simple versions (that really work!) of the instruments in a basic weather station. With your rain gauge, hygrometer, psychrometer, barometer, and anemometer, you'll be able to measure rainfall, barometric pressure, humidity, and wind speed. And you'll be analyzing information and making predictions, just as I do on the job as a weather forecaster every day.

So are you ready to take apart the weather to see what makes it tick, and start forecasting?

Mark S. Breen

WeaTher
IT's Everybody's Business!

We marvel at it, complain about it, and spend a lot of time trying to figure out what it's going to do next. Yes, **the weather** is always "news."

Farmers and **fishermen** depend on the weather to make a living. Poets are inspired by sunsets and sea breezes; we all know songs about **sunshine** and **rain**. The weather in your area affects whether you need to heat your house in winter, what kind of clothes you wear, even what kind of tires are on your car. Weather can change a school day to a "stay-home" day and determine when and where you go on vacation.

For every barbecue that's canceled by threatening **storm clouds**, there's a rainy morning that suddenly clears off so you can head for the **beach**. There's no doubt about it— the weather has a lot to do with how we live!

Let's Talk Weather

You might be surprised by all that you already know about the weather. After all, you've been living with it all your life!

Make a list of all the words you can think of that describe the weather and what it does. Here are some to get you started: sleet, downpour, drizzle . . .

Eyes on the Sky!

Did you know you've already got the most important tool you need to be a weather watcher?

A pair of sharp eyes! For hundreds of years, before there were instruments and equipment to measure the weather, people observed what the weather was doing, day in and day out, season after season. Patterns emerged over the years, and folks began to know what to expect (although there were always surprises!).

Meteorology is now an established science, but the basis of any science is still making careful observations and thinking about that information in terms of what you already know. That's how we understand the natural world and make discoveries.

WEATHER WORDS

Meteorology is the study of weather events, and **meteorologists** are scientists who predict the weather based on scientific data. These words both come from the Greek word *meteoron*, which means "thing in the heaven above."

ASK MARK!

What does a meteorologist do?

As a meteorologist, my job is to predict the weather and get that information out to people as a forecast (prediction). As you start your day, how do you know whether to put on a sweater or a T-shirt? How do farmers know if they can plant? The daily weather forecast helps answer these questions.

I get out of bed very early, because I start my workday around 4:30 AM, gathering weather reports, looking at satellite pictures and radar screens, checking computer weather data, and, believe it or not, even just looking out the window to try to figure out what the weather is going to do.

Then I write the forecast, choosing my words carefully to describe the weather situation as accurately as possible. Sometimes "partly sunny" is a good description of the weather, but sometimes "lots of clouds, with more sunny periods in the afternoon" is more accurate. My weather forecasts are used by several radio stations, a few newspapers, and even appear on the Eye on the Sky website at www.eotsweb.org.

When I'm not forecasting, I'm taking readings with weather instruments—or teaching weather and science in schools to kids like you!

Look for That...

Your softball game gets canceled because of rain. Or you're riding your bike to a friend's house when a little drizzle turns into icy rain or snow . . . ouch! We often think of weather in terms of "good" and "bad," and we tend to pay more attention to "bad" weather.

But what makes a day unpleasant for one person might make it comfortable, useful, or even beautiful to another. The same rain that ruins our softball games nourishes our lawns and gives us water to drink. The same sun that makes us squint and sweat also helps our gardens grow.

So, do you agree with the expression "Every cloud has a silver lining"? Is it about weather or about life?

...Silver Lining!

COLD WEATHER, WARM EARS!

In 1873, 15-year-old Chester Greenwood invented a weather beater that we still use today! When he went ice skating, his ears always got cold, but he was allergic to wool, so wearing a hat wasn't comfortable. So Chester made a wire frame with loops at each end that fit over his head, and his grandmother sewed fur on the outside of each loop and velvet on the inside. The "earflaps" worked so well that other kids were eager for a pair. By 1936, Chester had a factory that produced 400,000 earmuffs a year!

Try It: These days, all it takes is the push of a button or the turn of a dial to make the temperatures of our homes and cars more comfortable. With special fabrics like fleece and synthetics, we enjoy outdoor sports no matter what the weather. All these products came about because people like Chester set out to make life easier. If you were to invent a "weather beater," what might it be?

ASK MARK!

How would I know if I would enjoy being a meteorologist?

Do you like to read mysteries—and guess the ending before you finish the book? I think of a meteorologist as a kind of science detective. Meteorology is a science, so I studied lots of chemistry and physics in school. And even with all we know, the weather is not completely understood, so I have to use clues to figure out what it might do. I look at what the weather did in the past—last week or last year—to predict what I think will happen.

If you like observing all the amazing weather events that go on around us and using science to solve mysteries, you'd find being a meteorologist a very exciting job!

BE A METEOROLOGIST

KEEP A WEATHER LOG

Ready to start making observations about the weather where you live? To make a handy Weather Log, use a calendar with large spaces for writing and a three-ring binder with lined or graph paper. You can print out monthly calendars with many computer programs (or you can make your own) and use them to record daily observations. (Remember to date everything, so you can begin to see patterns emerge.)

Start with simple observations for each day: Is it windy or calm? Rainy or snowy? Sunny or partly sunny? Cloudy? (Draw what the clouds look like.)

As you go through this book, you'll make working versions of actual weather instruments.

You'll use this "weather station" to take detailed measurements of the weather and make predictions. Use your binder to record these measurements, along with comments and drawings.

HERE'S A WAY TO ORGANIZE YOUR WEATHER OBSERVATIONS AND MEASUREMENTS:

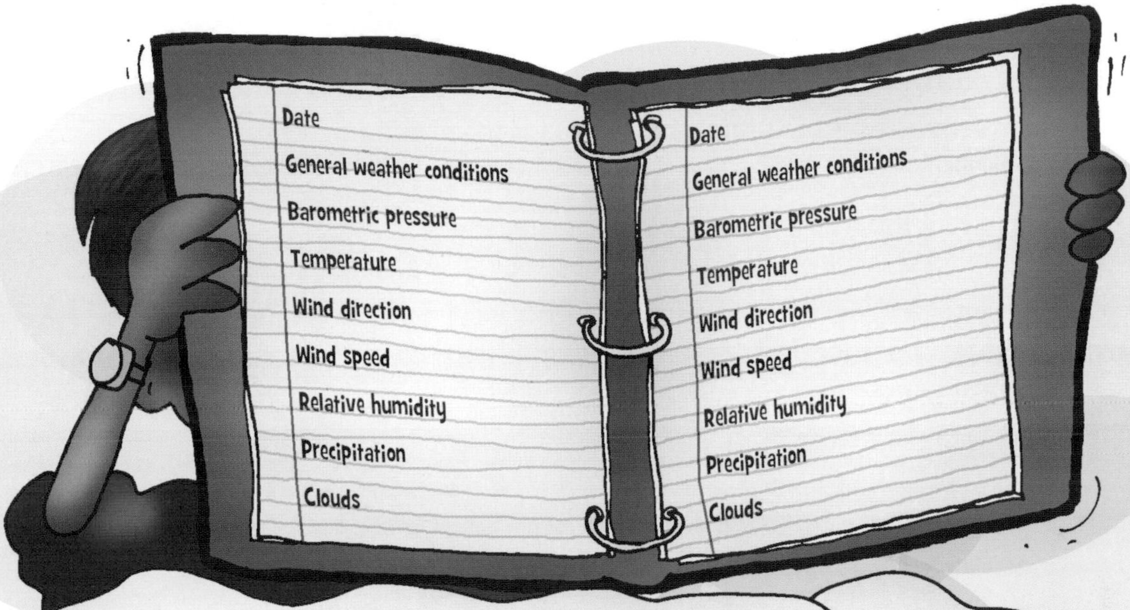

Date

General weather conditions

Barometric pressure

Temperature

Wind direction

Wind speed

Relative humidity

Precipitation

Clouds

Date

General weather conditions

Barometric pressure

Temperature

Wind direction

Wind speed

Relative humidity

Precipitation

Clouds

RECORD MORE DETAILED OBSERVATIONS AS WELL, CONSIDERING QUESTIONS LIKE THESE:

What did you wear?

How else did the weather affect your plans?

Was the weather the same in your backyard as it was on the school playground?

How did the weather change during the day?

Once you have a week or two of **data** (scientific information), you can start looking for weather patterns—relationships between a weather condition (wind from the northeast, for example) and the weather event that follows (rain later that day). Try writing a forecast for the next day's weather in your **log**—then see if you were right.

Can you . . .

Have you ever run outside in cold weather without your jacket, only to hear a grown-up say, "Put your coat on before you catch your death of cold!"? Can you really get sick from going outdoors without proper clothing, or "catch a chill" from wearing wet socks?

There is no medical evidence to support the idea that being out in cold weather will cause you to catch a cold. Colds are caught from people and not from cold weather. In fact, there is actually less chance of catching a cold in the cold: the virus that causes the common cold needs warmth to survive.

. . . caTch a coLd?

WHY IS IT CALLED GREENLAND?

Erik the Red, a Viking explorer, discovered Greenland, a huge island in the North Atlantic Ocean, about 1,000 years ago. Much of this island is farther north than Alaska and Siberia, so it is like one huge ice cap, with icebergs floating off the coast! The Vikings wanted settlers to come to this new land, but they knew people wouldn't rush to live in a place called Icebergland. So Erik the Red named this icy place Greenland to make it sound more appealing. Imagine the new settlers' surprise when they arrived to find only a narrow portion in the southern part where crops would grow! And today Greenland is colder! Almost all of it is covered with ice or *permafrost*, soil that stays frozen year-round.

What's your favorite part of your job?

I've always liked the fact that the weather is constantly changing—there's never a dull moment when you're a forecaster!

When serious weather conditions like an ice storm, a tornado, or a flood threaten people's safety, I feel good about doing special weather reports on the radio. It's exciting to watch and predict nature's most powerful storms, but what's even more rewarding is knowing I can give people important, useful information. And there's extra excitement when I am reporting "live" because if I make a mistake, thousands of people will hear it! I have to stay on my toes!

I'M A WEATHER POET

There came one drop of giant rain,
And Then, as if The hands
That held The dams had parted hold,
The waters wrecked The sky.
—Emily Dickinson

Can't you just see the downpour that Emily Dickinson describes in her poem about a thunderstorm called "The wind begun to rock the grass"? Weather creates some of the most dramatic scenes in nature—from a rosy pink sunset to a streak of lightning that seems to split the sky.

Describe your favorite weather scene and how it makes you feel in a weather poem. Maybe you love how fresh the world looks and smells after a spring shower, or the delicate patterns of frost on windowpanes on a winter morning. Use lots of descriptive words and let those feelings and images flow onto your paper. Collect your poems in your Weather Log.

WEATHER TUNES

Some weather-inspired songs have been big hits, like "Singin' in the Rain" (from the 1951 musical of the same name). Others, like Bob Dylan's "Blowin' in the Wind" or "Here Comes the Sun" by the Beatles, have turned up on the pop-music charts. And maybe you have a younger brother or sister who loves those old favorites, "Mr. Sun" and "Rain, Rain, Go Away."

Try It: How many songs and rhymes can you think of with the words sun, moon, rain, and showers in the title? Make a list in your Weather Log or have a competition with your friends to see who can name the most.

THE SINGING WEATHERMAN!

The weather even inspired Mark to write a song!

THE WEATHERMAN SONG
by Mark Breen

Who'd have ever thought I'd write a song about the weatherman?
Modern folkday hero who is trying to help us understand;
Weather isn't good or bad, and you can rest assured,
The only thing he's sure of is we're bound to have some more!

Think about your weatherman in radio or TV land,
Trying not to lose you with those terms that can confuse you!
He talks about his highs and lows, but they don't hold a feather
To looking out the window if you want to know the weather!

Here is my song dedicated to the weatherman,
Modern folkday hero who is trying to help us understand;
Weather isn't good or bad, it isn't right or wrong,
And if you'll just accept it, well, I think we'll get along!

Weathermen don't make the weather, they don't blow the snow,
They don't ask the clouds to come in, or the sun to go,
So if you hear the forecast and it's calling for rain,
Please believe the weatherman, he can't be wrong again!

Here is my song dedicated to the weatherman,
Modern folkday hero who is trying to help us understand;
Weather isn't good or bad, and you can rest assured,
The only thing he's sure of is we're bound to have some more!

(Look on page 136 for the music!)

The ATmosphere
An Ocean of Air

OK, hold your breath for this important announcement! You are at the bottom of an **ocean**—an ocean of **air**, that is!

Yes, the air you breathe is a lot like an ocean that surrounds the earth. We call this ocean of air the **atmosphere**. Not only does it provide the oxygen we need to breathe, but it protects us from the harsh environment of outer space.

The weather is like a huge machine that cranks out wind and rain, spins up storms, and pushes the clouds along to give us clear, sunny skies. Think of the atmosphere as the **engine** that runs this machine.

16

BARELY AWARE OF AIR

When you need to breathe, do you go looking for air? Of course not! It's just all around us. You might even forget that it's there. This stuff we call air is thinner and lighter than water.

Can you see air? Not exactly, but you can see the effects of air. Blow into a bag and quickly close the top. Could you flatten that bag without letting the air out? Although it's invisible, air has weight and takes up space, so it pushes out the sides of the bag.

Just how much air is up there?

Well, the air is "topless"—without a ceiling! The outer edge of the atmosphere blends into space, about 1,000 miles (1,600 km) above earth, where there is no air.

What keeps the atmosphere from just drifting away into outer space? The same force that holds us here on earth—gravity! Gravity is what gives everything, including us, its weight. The closer we are to earth, the stronger the force of gravity pulling us down. (Think about what happens to the astronauts when they get outside the pull of earth's gravity.)

The Pressure's On!

Using a sharp pencil or a nail, have a grownup help you poke three holes in the side of an empty half-gallon (2 L) cardboard milk carton. Holding the carton over the sink, fill it with water and watch how it leaks out of the holes. Does each stream of water look the same?

More water (so more weight) is pressing on the bottom hole, so the straightest stream is from the bottom hole. The water barely comes out the top hole because only a little water is pressing on top of the water leaking out.

It works the same way with air. The air closest to the earth has the weight of all the air above it pressing it down. This force is called **air pressure**. The farther you go up in the atmosphere, the less air pressure there is, because there's less and less air above pushing down.

ONE STRONG KID!

Does it seem funny to think of air weighing something? After all, we don't have to push it out of the way when we walk around. Well, not only does air have weight, but if we're at the bottom of this "ocean," where is most of the air? On top of us!

Put a sheet of notebook paper on the ground. Can you guess how much an amount of air that size would weigh? (Don't forget that air rises up in a column to the end of the atmosphere.) It weighs a whopping 1,293 pounds (582 kg)! So why doesn't it feel as if a herd of elephants is sitting on top of you? Your body is designed to handle the weight of the air. The pressure on the inside of your body (pushing out) adjusts to the pressure on the outside (pushing in) so they are equal. Now that's impressive!

What kind of weather puts the "pressure" on you when you're on the job?

My biggest challenge is when the weather is changing quickly—a line of dangerous thunderstorms forming rapidly on a summer afternoon, for example. Quickly responding and informing people of what may happen and how best to prepare can really be a matter of life or death.

Here in New England in the United States, winter weather really keeps me on my toes! Oftentimes, it will be snowing in one area, yet only a few miles away, freezing rain is falling instead. I have to be sure people are prepared for the conditions before they find themselves in a dangerous weather situation.

WEATHER AND WAR

Weather has often taken center stage in history, determining the outcome of major wars like the American Revolution.

General George Washington and his troops surprised the British by crossing the ice-choked Delaware River at midnight in December 1776. When the American forces reached the other side, they successfully struck enemy camps in Trenton, New Jersey, weakening the British army.

When Washington's troops camped at Valley Forge in Pennsylvania the following winter, they lacked the clothing and shelter necessary to spend the winter outside, and 2,000 of the 12,000 soldiers died. Just when it was beginning to look hopeless, the Americans rallied against the harsh weather. Additional supplies and equipment were sent to the camp. The American forces went on to win many battles—and the war!

What's the funniest weather saying you ever heard?

If ice in November will bear a duck,
Nothing comes after but sleet and muck.

I think ducks and muck are both funny, so it just sounds silly. However, the prediction is actually a pretty good one. Weather tends to go in cycles of cold, warm, cold, etc. So if the weather is cold enough in November to freeze the ponds (thick enough to hold up a duck), then the weather that follows in winter will be warmer than usual (sleet and muck!).

Your basic aneroid barometer

Make a Barometer

With tons and tons of air moving around all the time, a barometer is one of the most important tools meteorologists use to predict changes in the weather. You can make a simple version of an aneroid barometer that really works.

HERE'S WHAT YOU NEED:

- **Petroleum jelly**
- **Empty can without top**
- **Balloon**
- **Rubber band**
- **Tape**
- **Drinking straw**
- **Light-colored poster board**
- **Marker**

HERE'S WHAT YOU DO:

1 Spread a thin layer of petroleum jelly around the edge of the can (be careful not to cut yourself). Stretch the uninflated balloon over the can and seal it with a rubber band.

2 Tape a straw onto the middle of the balloon.

3 Place a piece of folded poster board next to the can in a place where it won't be disturbed. Mark the end of the straw on the poster board.

4 Check your barometer once or twice or day for a week, and mark any changes in position. Label your highest mark "High" and your lowest mark "Low."

READING YOUR BAROMETER

Air pressure changes from day to day as weather systems travel over or near you.

- **When air warms up**, it gets lighter and rises. When this happens over an area of hundreds of miles/km (the state where you live, for example), there is less air pressing down on the balloon. The air inside the can pushes up, causing the end of the straw to move *down*, indicating that the air pressure is *falling*. Low pressure brings stormy weather.

- **As air cools down,** it becomes heavier and sinks, so more is pressing down on the balloon. How does this affect the straw? What does that tell you about the air pressure? What kind of weather do you think you should look for?

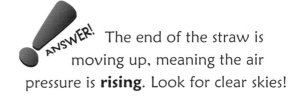

ANSWER! The end of the straw is moving up, meaning the air pressure is **rising**. Look for clear skies!

METEOROLOGIST

BAROMETRIC UPS & DOWNS

In your Weather Log, record the position of the straw every day and then describe the weather.

Do you notice any relationship between the position of the barometer and the weather? Clear and sunny? Overcast?

On many liquid barometers, you'll find words describing the weather next to the column of mercury that records the air pressure. Lower pressure is often labeled "stormy" or "rain," while higher pressure is described as "fair" or "dry." In between is generally labeled "change."

Try It: On your poster board, label the low-pressure area "rainy," the high-pressure "sunny," and in between "change." Do your barometer readings always match the actual weather?

FORECASTER'S "GETTING IT RIGHT" RULES!

- When the barometric pressure is high, skies are fair, and it's a great day to be outside.

- When air pressure is falling, watch out! Wet or stormy weather is on the way.

- If the pressure is "steady," as forecasters say, then no change in the weather is predicted.

Try It: Here's an easy way to remember this: Point your thumb in the direction that the barometer (and the air pressure) is changing. If the barometer is going up, the weather gets a "thumbs up." If the pressure is falling, the weather gets a "thumbs down," meaning stormy weather.

BE A
METEOROLOGIST

CHOOSE YOUR BALLPARK

You've won tickets to see the Chicago Cubs play the Colorado Rockies, and you get to choose whether to watch the game at Wrigley Field in Chicago or at Coors Field in Denver. You really want to see your favorite slugger hit a homer. The Denver game is tomorrow; the Chicago game is next week. It has been partly cloudy in both cities, and the barometer is steady. Chicago is only about 500 feet (154 m) above sea level, and Denver's nickname is the "Mile High City"! In which stadium do you have a better chance of seeing the ball blasted out of the park?

(Hint: Think about elevation and air pressure.)

ANSWER! **Root for your team in Denver.** More baseballs make it over the fence in Denver than at lower elevations like Chicago. The air pressure in Denver, which is one mile (1.6 km) above sea level, is lower than the pressure at lower elevations. This means there is a little less air to push through, so things like baseballs can fly farther. And with a steady barometer, no major storms are brewing to threaten your favorite slugger's chances.

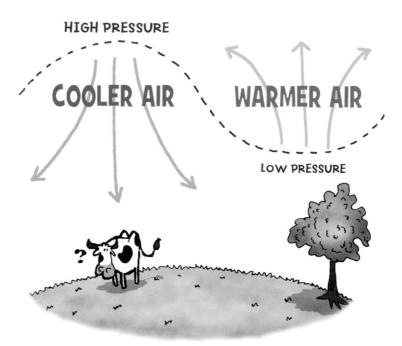

WEATHER WORDS

A large mass of low-pressure air is called a **low**. What do you think forecasters call a large area of high-pressure air?

So when the weather forecaster says, "Look for a high-pressure area to move in by Wednesday morning," that means Wednesday will be nice?

Almost always.

Then why not just say, "Look for a beautiful day on Wednesday"?

Well, air pressure is only one part of the weather. Other parts like the temperature, the wind, and the humidity may have different effects. Barometric pressure is a great measurement to start with, though. We'll add more tools and forecasting information in the next few chapters.

HIGH PRESSURE

COOLER AIR   WARMER AIR

LOW PRESSURE

ANSWER! A large area of high-pressure air is called a **high**.

QUICK-TAKE ? FORECASTS

1. It's a beautiful sunny morning, and you're planning a picnic for later in the day. You notice that your barometer is falling. Will it stay sunny?

2. Yesterday at 10 AM your thermometer read 42°F (5.5°C), and today at 10 AM it reads 46°F (7.7°C). What do you think your barometer is doing? Should you take your raincoat when you go out?

ANSWERS! 1. Not likely. Falling pressure often indicates a storm approaching.

2. Warmer, lighter air is starting to arrive, causing the air pressure to fall, and the barometer to drop. This could mean rain, so grab your slicker.

You're acting just like...

Would people say you have a sunny disposition? Do two friends who have a lot of ups and downs have a stormy relationship?

Sometimes we use images of weather events to describe people. What do we say about someone who doesn't pay attention and is daydreaming?

...the weather!

HE HAS HIS HEAD IN THE CLOUDS.

Why does the sky look blue?

Well, for starters, think about when it looks blue. Is it blue when it's cloudy or raining? Is it blue at night? So our blue sky has something to do with . . . sunlight!

Put a mirror in a glass of water so the mirror is at an angle and facing the sun. Hold a piece of paper at a slant in front of the glass. Move the paper until seven colors show up clearly on your paper. (Recognize those colors?) Although it appears to be white (or colorless), light is really made up of seven visible colors. You used the mirror and the water to bend, or refract, the sunlight so it separated into those seven colors, called the spectrum.

As a beam of sunlight travels through the atmosphere, most of the colors of the spectrum pass directly to earth. Some of the blue light, however, hits particles of air and is scattered across the sky, making it look blue.

 WEATHER WATCHERS | Lord John William Strutt Rayleigh

This English scientist asked himself that same question: why is the sky blue? He won the Nobel Prize in 1904 for discovering how light rays scatter when they pass through air, making the sky appear blue.

ROY G. BIV!

On a bright sunny day, grab the garden hose. Standing with your back to the sun, spray a fine mist so that the sunlight shines right through the water. You made your own rainbow!

What's more, you now know how that rainbow was created! When the sunlight bounces off the droplets of water, it is separated into the spectrum, and we see the colors of a rainbow: red, orange, yellow, green, blue, indigo, and violet—or ROY G. BIV!

Howdy! I'm ROY G. BIV!

Red sky at night, sailor's delight. Red sky at morning, sailors take warning.

Here's an excellent example of how making careful observations (the color of the sunset and the sunrise) and then connecting them to the type of weather that follows can be a reliable way of forecasting. People have been watching these natural events for thousands of years, and over time they noticed that the most colorful sunsets were followed by sunny, dry weather (good news for sailors), while a beautiful sunrise almost always came ahead of a storm (sailors, be careful). This saying is true about **80 percent** of the time, or four out of five days.

UNDERSTANDING PERCENTS

Percent (%) comes from the Latin *per centum*, or "in every hundred." If we say this weather saying is true 80 percent of the time, we mean that it forecasts the weather correctly 80 out of every 100 times. Not too bad!

Meteorologists often use percentages to indicate the likelihood of the weather doing something. For example, they might say, "There's a 75 percent chance of showers tomorrow." Hmmm . . . should you take your raincoat?

You mean... You're not sure?

SCIENCE IN THE SKY

Thanks to modern science, we now know that the red color at sunset or sunrise comes from the sun's spectrum (see page 29). At the beginning or end of the day, when the sun appears lower in the sky, its rays pass through more of the dust and other small particles normally found in the atmosphere. These particles filter the sun's light, knocking out the violets, blues, and greens of the spectrum, but letting the yellows, oranges, and reds through.

If we see a colorful sunset, then we can be sure there is dust in the air. And if there is dust, then it is not raining (rain would wash the dust particles out of the air). Also, if we can see the sun setting, we know there are not many clouds. So, we can pretty safely say the weather to the west is dry and pleasant. Over the centuries, weather watchers have noticed that most weather systems come from the west and move toward the east. So, tomorrow's weather should be a sailor's delight.

Red skies in the morning mean the delightful weather is already to the east of you, and moving away. This nice weather is most often followed by stormy weather, which is why "red sky at morning, sailors take warning!"

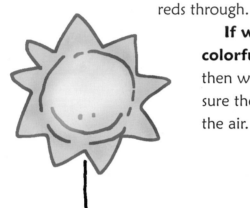

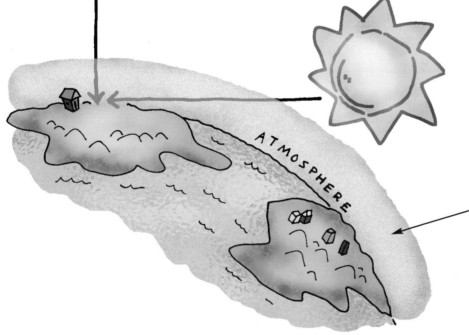

ATMOSPHERE

When the sun is low on the horizon, its light must travel farther through the atmosphere than during the day, when the sun is right overhead.

Dust and other small particles

The Energetic Sun

So what's the **fuel** that "powers" this big weather machine? The **sun!** (Without the sun, there would be no weather, because everything would be frozen!)

The sun's **energy** doesn't warm the earth and its atmosphere evenly, however. Clouds can **block** the sun in one place while it shines brightly a few miles away, for example. Ice and snow reflect the sun's **heat** back into space, while areas of bare soil **soak up** the heat. These different locations of heat and cold are what make temperature, air pressure, wind speed, cloud formation—in other words, the weather!—change from day to day in most parts of the world.

Forecasters study these differences in the amount of heat earth receives to determine how strong storms and other weather systems will be.

Fuel from Far, Far Away!

The sun sends enormous amounts of energy out into space in every direction, but we're so many millions of miles away, we get only a tiny, tiny amount of it. The sun's energy is so great, however, that even the small amount that reaches earth is more energy than we use in all the world's cars, houses, and factories combined!

Sunny day...

Does a beautiful sunny day make your spirits soar? How about a dark winter day—does it make you feel as gloomy as the weather? As you record weather conditions in your log, keep track of your moods also—do you notice any mood patterns? Now, try tracking your parents' moods and see if they change with the weather. It will help you choose just the right time to ask about getting that new puppy!

...sunny mood?

BE A
METEOROLOGIST

TAKING THE TEMPERATURE

"Phew! It's hot!" "Brrr! I'm chilly!"
Temperature is probably the weather condition we respond to most frequently. It's also one of the easiest weather measurements to record accurately at home. We measure the temperature of the air around us using a thermometer that reads in degrees Fahrenheit or Celsius (see page 35).

You may already have an outdoor

thermometer at home. If not, a small portable one is great (very inexpensive at a hardware store), because you can compare temperature readings between sunny and shady locations.

Record your daily readings in your Weather Log, below the barometer readings. If possible, record the temperature early in the day (as close to sunrise as possible), and again in the afternoon (around 2:30 PM in the winter and around 4 PM in the summer). These readings will be close to the lowest and highest temperatures for each day. After recording your temperatures for a week or more, can you see a relationship between higher and lower barometric pressure and temperature?

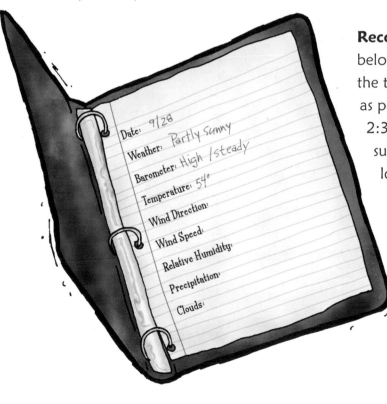

Date: 9/28
Weather: Partly Sunny
Barometer: High /steady
Temperature: 54°
Wind Direction:
Wind Speed:
Relative Humidity:
Precipitation:
Clouds:

1. It's a cloudy winter morning and the barometer is rising. Do you forecast warmer or colder weather for the afternoon?

2. It's 10 AM. Your thermometer reads 55°F (13°C), the barometric pressure is rising, and the sun is shining brightly. You wonder if you'll be able to fly your kite this afternoon, or will rain ruin your plans?

ANSWERS! 1. Colder weather is on the way, because the rising barometer means heavier, colder air is moving in. There is no sunshine to counter the effect of this cold air.

2. As the day goes on, the sun will warm the chilly air and the high pressure will keep the rain away. It should be a great afternoon for kite flying!

FAHRENHEIT AND CELSIUS

Celsius is the standard form of measurement used worldwide by scientists, as well as in most countries for everyday use. In 1742, Anders Celsius, a Swedish astronomer, developed the following temperature scale: the temperature at which fresh water freezes is called 0°C, and the point at which it boils is called 100°C. Then, he divided that range into an equal number of degrees. This scale is named after him, and it is also called *centigrade* (*centi* means 100).

Fahrenheit is another temperature scale still commonly used in the United States. In 1714, the Polish scientist Gabriel Fahrenheit made the first mercury thermometer using this measurement scale: the point where a mixture of water and alcohol freezes is 0°F; the point where fresh water freezes is 32°F; and the point where it boils is 212°F.

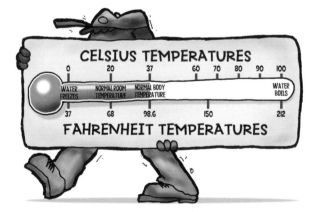

CALLING ALL MATH WIZARDS!

Here's how to convert (change) degrees Celsius (C) to degrees Fahrenheit (F).

> **Multiply the temperature in °C by 9**
> **Divide the answer by 5**
> **Add 32**

1. So when the Celsius thermometer reads 33°, what's the Fahrenheit temperature?

To go the other way, just reverse the steps.

> **Subtract 32 from the temperature in °F**
> **Multiply by 5**
> **Divide by 9**

Need an Answer Quick?
For a shortcut, here's how to estimate:

> **-10°C = 15°F (really 14°F)**
> **0°C = 30°F (really 32°F)**
> **10°C = 50°F**
> **20°C = 70°F (really 68°F)**
> **30°C = 85°F (really 86°F)**

2. So, if it is 5°C, it is how many degrees F?

ANSWERS! 1. 33 x 9 = 297; 297 ÷ 5 = 59 (rounded to nearest degree); 59 + 32 = 91°F. Whew! It's a hot day!

2. You would estimate 40°F. 5°C is halfway between 0° and 10°C, so your answer is 40°F, halfway between 30° and 50°F. If you calculated the answer, it would be 41°F—pretty close!

BE A
METEOROLOGIST

AVERAGE HIGHS AND LOWS

As you follow your temperatures for one to two weeks, you are building an important forecasting tool. Forecasters know that the temperature rises and falls about the same amount every day. It changes slightly, of course, depending on how much sun is shining, or whether a warm or cold wind is blowing, but it's still a very helpful measurement to track.

How can you figure out the temperature rise and fall for your location? You'll need to do a little math using the readings in your Weather Log.

1 Add up all of the daily high temperatures; then, divide by the number of days (if you add up 10 days of temperatures, then divide by 10). The answer is the average high temperature for that period of time.

2 Now, do the same with the daily low temperatures to get the average low temperature.

3 Subtract the average low from the average high. This is the average amount the temperature rises and falls each day.

FORECASTER'S "GETTING IT RIGHT" RULES!

- The difference between the highest and the lowest temperatures of the day in any specific place is always about the same during each particular season—spring, summer, fall, or winter.

- This figure predicts how the temperature will change during the day.

❶
```
  70
  68
  72
+ 67
  73
─────
 350
```
5 DAYS?
DIVIDE BY 5!
```
     70
 5 )350
```
$70° =$ AVERAGE HIGH TEMP

❷
```
  42
  40
  42
+ 51
  40
─────
 215
```
5 DAYS?
DIVIDE BY 5!
```
     43
 5 )215
```
$43° =$ AVERAGE LOW TEMP

❸
```
  70  AVERAGE HIGH
- 43  AVERAGE LOW
─────
  27° = AVERAGE
       AMOUNT OF
       TEMP RISE
       AND FALL
```

1. Your average rise in the temperature is 20°F (11°C). This morning, the temperature is 40°F (4°C). What do you forecast the afternoon temperature to be?

2. This morning's temperature is 50°F (10°C), and you forecast the afternoon temperature to be 60°F (15°C). On your barometer, the air pressure is falling. Will tomorrow be warmer or colder?

ANSWERS! 1. This afternoon, the temperature will be 60°F (15°C). 40°F/4°C (current temperature) + 20°F/11°C (average daily rise) = 60°F/15°C (afternoon temperature).

2. Things should warm up even more tomorrow, because falling air pressure indicates that warmer air is moving toward the region. However, clouds and rain could affect your forecast.

No Thermometer? Just use a...

Count the number of times a cricket chirps in a 13-second period; then add 40. That number will come close to the actual temperature in degrees Fahrenheit most of the time. Really! Try it!

...cricket!

Which Hemisphere Are You In?

Put a rubber band around the middle of a ball from left to right. The band is just like the **Equator**, an imaginary line that divides the earth into two halves, the Northern and Southern Hemispheres (hemi=half; sphere=ball). Picture a band dividing the ball the other way (up and down). Now you are looking at the Eastern and Western Hemispheres. Do you know which hemisphere North America is in?

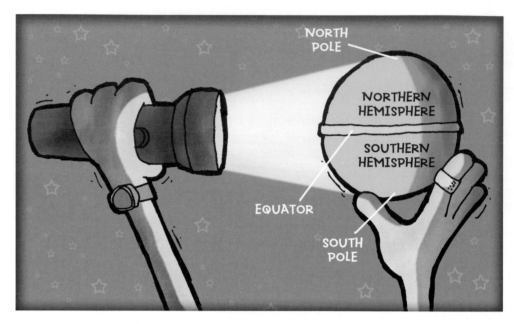

NORTH POLE

NORTHERN HEMISPHERE

SOUTHERN HEMISPHERE

EQUATOR

SOUTH POLE

Now, shine a flashlight on the ball as shown. Notice how the light shines on the rubber band, compared with the way it shines on the top and bottom of the ball. Rotate the ball without moving the flashlight. Does the way the light hits the rubber band change as the ball turns?

The Equator always receives more of the sun's energy than the poles. With all that hot air, the equator is usually an area of low pressure (see pages 23–24). See how much less of the sun's heat hits the North and South Poles (the top and bottom of your ball)? These regions are always cold, so they are almost always areas of high pressure.

ANSWER! North America is in the **Northern** and **Western** Hemispheres.

THE REASON FOR THE SEASONS

Notice how the earth is always at a tilt as it *orbits* (moves completely around) the sun? Although the equator receives a constant amount of heat from the sun, because of this angle, the rest of the earth receives different amounts of the sun's energy—and this creates our four seasons.

When the Northern Hemisphere is tilted toward the sun, it receives more hours of daylight and stronger sunlight—and the people living there have summer. Meanwhile, in the Southern Hemisphere, it's winter. See how the Northern Hemisphere is tilted away from the sun during its winter? At that time, the days are shorter and the sunlight is not as intense because it is lower in the sky. Meanwhile, the Southern Hemisphere is enjoying long, warm summer days.

In the spring and fall, the earth is not leaning toward or away from the sun, so it is neither very hot nor very cold. But there is a lot of mixing of warm and cold air during those seasons. All that unsettled air means strong thunderstorms and sometimes hail and tornadoes for many parts of North America.

As a forecaster, what season do you enjoy the most?

I enjoy them all. If the earth just stayed in one place, our weather would be the same all year (and I'd be out of a job!). But with the earth always moving around the sun, here in North America the changing weather conditions that make up our seasons keep things interesting for me as a weather forecaster.

SPRING

SUMMER

WINTER

FALL

A Cape for ALL Seasons

Celebrate the seasons with a weather collage you can wear!

HERE'S WHAT YOU NEED:
- **An old sheet**
- **Marker**
- **Scissors**
- **Tape measure**
- **Decorations (see step 3)**
- **Glue**

HERE'S WHAT YOU DO:

1 Wrap the sheet around your shoulders like a cape. Ask a friend to mark with the marker where the sheet hits the floor (leave extra material in back so it will drag a little). Cut along the mark (discard the excess).

2 In the center of the top edge, about 2" (5 cm) in from the edge of the sheet, draw a circle that's 10" (25 cm) in diameter (ask a grownup to help). Cut out the hole.

3 With the marker and tape measure, divide your cape into four sections of equal size. Using old magazines and newpapers, fabric scraps, nature "finds," and markers, glue on decorations appropriate for each season: beachballs and a big sun for summer; photos of skiers or headlines about snow and ice for winter; leaves for fall.

WEATHER LORE

GROUNDHOG DAY

What animal tells us whether spring will be early or late? The **groundhog**, of course! Groundhog Day (February 2) was first celebrated by farmers in Germany, who then brought the tradition to the United States. According to longtime legend, if the groundhog wakes up from hibernating and comes out of his den only to be frightened by his shadow, he'll crawl back in, and there will be six more weeks of winter. If he doesn't see his shadow, spring is on the way.

ASK MARK!

Is there any truth to Groundhog Day?

As a weather predictor, the groundhog is wrong more than he's right, but don't blame him! People probably didn't watch the groundhog for years, and connect his behavior with a weather event, the way they did with sunrises and sunsets (see pages 29–30). Instead, Groundhog Day started in Europe, where it had many names, but one date. February 2 is the traditional half-way mark between the first day of winter and the first day of spring. In France, there were traditions of bears coming out of their caves, and in Germany, farmers watched for badgers. There is a lot of tradition and fun, but no science.

HEY! DON'T BLAME ME!

Catch Some Rays!

HERE'S WHAT YOU NEED:
- **Thermometer**
- **2 aluminum pie pans: 1 filled with water, 1 filled with soil**

HERE'S WHAT YOU DO:

Place the pans in a sunny spot. For several days, measure the temperature of the water and the soil (allow the thermometer to return to the starting point between measurements). Take readings in the morning and at the end of the day, and record your measurements in your Weather Log. Which pan has the higher temperature? Which pan changes the most when the sun goes down?

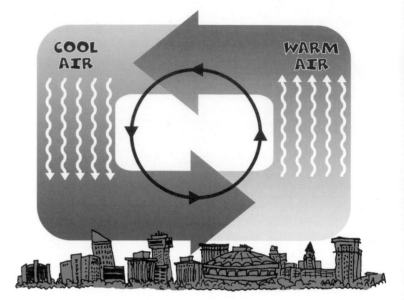

Firing Up the Weather Machine!

Dark colors and heavy materials, like soil or pavement, absorb (soak up) the sun's heat. Light colors and softer materials, like water or grass, reflect (send back) some of that heat into the atmosphere.

The air temperature over a place that absorbs the heat is higher than it is over places that reflect it. Air keeps moving from these cool, high-pressure spots to warmer, low-pressure ones, trying to even things out. These up-and-down movements, called convection currents, occur all over the earth. It's the sun's energy, powering our weather!

FORECASTER'S "GETTING IT RIGHT" RULES!

- The sun's energy creates changes in air temperature, which in turn, cause changes in air pressure.

- Remember: Warm air rises like a balloon; when it gets cold, it will sink again soon!

- Rising air currents are the primary source of energy for storms.

WeaTher...

Convection currents are invisible, but a feathered friend can help you see them at work. Hawks often take advantage of these rising currents to lift them higher with less effort. If you watch hawks soaring high in the sky, you'll see that they glide for long distances without flapping their wings, riding these currents of warm air.

...on The wing

KEEP YOUR COOL! On a hot, sunny day, walk barefoot across the grass. Now walk on some asphalt. What do you notice? Take a brisk walk in a black or dark-colored T-shirt. Then try it wearing a white one. Which is more comfortable? Why?

QUICK-TAKE ❓ FORECASTS

1. You are in charge of planning your school's Welcome-to-Spring Ice Cream Party, held outdoors every year. Considering what you know about different surfaces and the sun (and what you know about ice cream!), where on the school grounds should you hold the party? What time of day would be best? What should you do if the sunrise is red on the morning of the event (see pages 25–26)?

2. You are planning your family's annual summer reunion at your favorite park. There are two pavilions you can choose from. One is conveniently located next to the parking lot, which is paved. The second one is farther away, but it is next to the lake and surrounded by grass. Both offer shade. Where are people going to be more comfortable?

ANSWERS! 1. Avoid setting up your tables near the school buildings or on pavement, because those surfaces absorb heat—you'll be cooler on the soccer field. Start your party early in the morning (the coolest part of the day). If the sky is red at sunrise, uh-oh! Be prepared to move the event indoors.

2. Although shade will keep both locations comfortable, the pavilion near the lake will be a little cooler. The water helps to cool the air, and so does the grass. The paved parking lot adds to the heat, so the pavilion next to it could get pretty uncomfortable on a hot summer day.

Aaahh...

Why does the news make such a big fuss about heat waves?

Hot weather can make it harder to breathe, and extreme heat makes your heart work harder to help cool off your body. Older people and people with health problems related to breathing and heart conditions need to take special care on hot days—not too much sun or moving around.

Drinking lots of water and staying inside (especially if it's air-conditioned) help. When the temperature soars, make a point of checking on older relatives and neighbors to make sure they are comfortable—they'll appreciate it!

DOIN' OKAY?

WEATHER RECORDS

The **hottest** temperature in North America was measured in Death Valley, California, at 134°F (57°C), on July 10, 1913. It is very close to the world's record of 136°F (58°C) recorded in the Sahara Desert of northern Africa in 1922.

Wind
Always Stirring Things Up

So our ocean of **air** has currents moving through it, just like an ocean of water! Thanks to differences in the way the sun's energy heats the earth, these **convection currents** occur throughout the atmosphere, as cool, high-pressure air mixes with warm, low-pressure air.

Can you guess another name for this moving air? **Wind!**

What makes wind strong or gentle? Warm or cold? And how does it affect our weather?

Make a Wind Vane

Meteorologists describe wind direction by noting where the wind is blowing from—and that's the direction your wind vane will point in. So if the weather report calls for southerly winds, which way will your wind vane point? How about if the forecast is for "winds south to southeast"?

Leave a hole for the pen cap

HERE'S WHAT YOU NEED:
- **Tagboard or cardboard, roughly 8" x 24" (20 cm x 60 cm)**
- **Pencil and markers**
- **Scissors**
- **Glue or tape**
- **Pen cap**
- **Wire coat hanger**

HERE'S WHAT YOU DO:

1 Fold the tagboard in half and draw an outline of an arrow on it. Draw a bird in the center as shown, if you like. Cut out the shape.

2 Glue the two pieces together, leaving a small opening as shown. Draw features on the bird.

3 Glue or tape the pen cap into the opening, making sure the cap is level. Flatten the "hook" of the hanger and insert it into the cap.

4 Now, head outside with your wind vane. Bend the rest of the hanger around a fence post or block of wood.

5 Stand nearby facing west (the direction you look in to watch the sun set) with your arms outstretched. Your left hand is pointing south, and your right hand is pointing north. What direction is behind you? East, of course! Watch your wind vane to see what direction the wind is blowing from.

ANSWERS! 1) Your wind vane will point south.

2) The direction the wind is blowing from is ranging from the south to the southeast, so your wind vane will range between those directions.

FORECASTER'S "GETTING IT RIGHT" RULES!

- Wind usually brings along the kind of weather typical of the place the wind comes from. A north wind is cold because it started in a colder place; a south wind brings warm air from down south.

Where I live in the northeastern United States, there are a lot of weather vanes on barn roofs. Are weather vanes and wind vanes the same thing? Why did farmers need them?

Farmers are very sharp weather watchers, because they need to know what kinds of weather are headed for their fields. A north wind signals colder weather that could indicate a chance of frost in the spring or the fall. A warm, dry wind from the southwest could bring just the right weather to help dry the hay before putting it in the barn. Because wind vanes give such a strong indication of the weather to follow, people also call them weather vanes.

BE A METEOROLOGIST

WIND DIRECTION AND WEATHER

For the next week, observe the wind direction (several times a day, if possible). Record your observations in your Weather Log.

Compare the wind direction with the other weather data you've been recording. When the wind changes direction, what kind of changes do you notice taking place in the weather?

Date: 8/29
Weather: THUNDERSTORM
Barometer: LOW and FALLING
Temperature: 78°F 25°C
Wind Direction: Southwest
Wind Speed:
Relative Humidity:
Precipitation:
Clouds:

WEATHER WORDS

A sudden, violent wind that often carries rain or snow and makes it difficult to see is a **squall**.

Wind, What Are You Bringing Us?

Check your log and see if your observations match this chart.

IF THE WIND COMES FROM THESE DIRECTIONS:	AND THE AIR PRESSURE IS:	YOU SHOULD PREDICT:
East, Northeast, or North	Low, falling fast	Windy with heavy rain or snow; clearing after 24 hours
South, Southeast, or East	Low, falling fast	Windy with heavy rain, or snow changing to rain, clearing within 24 hours
South or Southwest	Low, rising slowly	Clearing, fair for 2 to 3 days
Shifting to West	Low, rising fast	Storm ends, clearing and colder
Southeast, East, or Northeast	Falling slowly	Rain/snow starting soon, lasting 1 to 2 days
East or Northeast	Falling slowly	Rain/snow within 24 hours
Southeast, East, or Northeast	Falling fast	Rain/snow in 12 hours, clearing in 36 hours
Southwest, West, or Northwest	High, rising fast	Fair, then warmer with rain/snow in 2 days
Southwest, West, or Northwest	High, rising slowly	Fair, little change in temperature for 1 to 2 days
Southwest, West, or Northwest	High, falling slowly	Fair with slowly rising temperatures for 1 to 2 days

1. The barometric pressure is rising. It's raining and the wind is from the northwest. The temperature is 75°F (24°C). Will it continue to rain for a long or short time? Do you expect it to get warmer, colder, or stay the same?

QUICK-TAKE FORECASTS

2. The barometer has been steady, at fairly high pressure, for the past two days, but this morning the wind direction changed from northwest to east-northeast. The temperature on this sunny day is 35°F (2°C). What is in store for tomorrow?

3. On Friday morning, it is raining hard and the trees in your backyard are swaying to the north, with big winds howling away. What do you think your barometer will show? What will the weather be like this weekend?

ANSWERS! 1. The rain will end soon because the rising barometer indicates the storm is moving away and the northwest wind is bringing drier air. The temperature is likely to drop because a northwest wind comes from cooler places to your north and west. This won't always be true in the summer, however. The clouds and rain can make the air cooler, but when the sun comes out, the temperature will rise.

2. Steady pressure means any storm is not close yet. Winds changing to the east and northeast mean a winter storm may be on its way in 24 to 48 hours (one to two days). If so, clouds will keep the sun hidden tomorrow and make the temperatures a little colder, meaning the moisture will likely come in the form of snow.

3. The air pressure is low and falling fast. When pressure falls fast, the storm is usually moving quickly, so look for clearing and breezy on Saturday, and fair weather Sunday.

Follow That Drop!

Dust the upper half of a ball with a thin layer of flour or chalk dust. Now, spin your "earth" east to west (clockwise). While it's spinning, put a drop of water (for the wind) near the "North Pole." After a few seconds, stop the ball.

What do you notice about the path of the water?

Earth's rotation

High pressure rotates counter-clockwise in the Northern Hemisphere

High pressure rotates clockwise in the Northern Hemisphere

Equator

Low pressure rotates clockwise in the Northern Hemisphere

Low pressure rotates counter-clockwise in the Northern Hemisphere

Putting a Spin on the Wind

While air is moving from higher pressure to lower pressure, the earth is turning beneath it. This rotation causes winds to curve in circular patterns (just the way spinning the ball caused the water drop to follow a curved path).

In the Northern Hemisphere, the winds are pushed to the right, and in the Southern Hemisphere, they're pushed to the left. This is called the *Coriolis* (CORE-ee-oh-lis) *effect*, named after Gustave-Gaspard de Coriolis, the French scientist who discovered it.

FORECASTER'S "GETTING IT RIGHT" RULES!

IN THE NORTHERN HEMISPHERE:

- Winds go clockwise (the same direction as the hands on a clock) around areas of high pressure.

- Winds go counter-clockwise (the opposite of a clock) around areas of low pressure.

Try It: Stand with your back to the wind, holding your arms outstretched. Your left hand will be pointing to a low-pressure area: a storm.

Your right hand is pointing to a high-pressure area with drier air. What kind of weather will you find there?

IN THE SOUTHERN HEMISPHERE:

- The rules work exactly the opposite way.

 Your right hand is pointing in the direction of **fair weather**.

I love the beach. Even on a really hot day with the sun out, it feels cooler and more comfortable there. How's that?

Even if you don't go swimming, you're still cooled by that refreshing sea breeze. Ahhh! As you saw with your pans of soil and water (see page 42), the sun heats up land faster than water. This means there is cooler, heavier (high-pressure) air over the water, and warmer, lighter (low-pressure) air over the land. Remember, air always goes from more pressure to less pressure, so it blows from the cooler water to the warmer land.

But hang out on the beach until early evening. Do you notice a change? The water holds the warmth longer than the land, so now it's the air above the water that's warmer and lighter, with low pressure. Predict how this change will affect the air flow.

ANSWER! The wind now moves from the land out over the water, creating a land breeze.

A narrow band of high-speed wind that blows from west to east in the upper atmosphere is called the **jet stream**. It's so strong it steers entire weather systems! Scientists use **weather balloons** (helium balloons that carry weather instruments and transmit data back to earth) to locate and track the jet stream because it gives forecasters an important tool to predict the direction of storms.

RECORDED IN HISTORY

A REAL BOOST!

In the 1940s, during the Second World War, pilots traveling between Alaska and Japan noticed a curious thing. The flight to Japan was much longer than the return trip! Scientists discovered a very strong wind blowing between 35,000 and 60,000 feet (10,769 and 18,461 m) above the earth. It gave jet airplanes traveling in the same direction an extra boost, so it was called the jet stream.

Make an Anemometer

Here is a simple version of a rotation anemometer that you can use to observe changes in wind speed.

HERE'S WHAT YOU NEED:

- **Scissors**
- **Large plastic cup**
- **Pencil with eraser**
- **Packing tape**
- **4 small paper cups**
- **Stapler**
- **2 straws**
- **Square of sturdy cardboard**
- **Push pin**

Staple here

HERE'S WHAT YOU DO:

1 Poke a hole through the bottom of the large cup so that the pencil will slide through. Tape the cup to the cardboard and push the pencil through the hole.

2 Cut off the tops of the small cups so they're about 1" (2.5 cm) deep. Make an identifying mark on one of the cups. Tape or staple a cup onto each end of the straws, one facing in one direction and one facing in the other.

3 Staple the straws into an X shape and attach them to the pencil eraser with the push pin.

4 Set your anemometer outside (put some rocks on the cardboard to steady it if necessary). Observe your anemometer in several situations and each time, record the number of revolutions the marked cup makes in one minute. Now you have a basis for knowing whether the wind is picking up or slowing down.

An **anemometer** measures wind speed in miles per hour (or kilometers per hour). A **rotation anemometer**, standard equipment in most weather stations, has three or more cone-shaped cups that rotate on a pivot. The number of rotations per minute translates to a certain wind speed.

How high does the wind go? Does an airplane pilot flying at 30,000 feet (9,230 m) have to worry about wind direction and speed?

Strong winds can be found up to 70,000 feet (21,358 m). The air way up there is so thin that it's difficult for aircraft to fly much higher. Pilots need to pay special attention to the winds. A pilot can ride the wind the same way a raft rides currents in a river, getting from one place to another more quickly and using less fuel. However, if the winds aren't favorable, pilots avoid them because they slow the plane down too much.

How does wind speed affect your forecast?

Because the wind brings air from one place to another, knowing where the air is coming from gives me a good clue about what kind of weather to predict. Strong winds also affect many outdoor activities, like sailing, hiking, biking, baseball, and football. And they can be dangerous—knocking down tree limbs and power lines, or causing snowdrifts on the roads—so I need to warn people whenever high winds might create hazardous conditions.

Breeze or gale?

In 1806, Sir Francis Beaufort (BO-furt), an English admiral, came up with a method of measuring wind speed on a scale of 1 to 12 by observing the effect of wind on a fully rigged sailing ship. The scale was named after him, and later, descriptions of wind effects on land were added.

...check The Beaufort ScaLe!

0 CaLm
Smokes rises
0 mph (0 kph)

1 LighT air
Smoke drifts
1–3 mph (1–5 kph)

2 SLighT breeze
Leaves rustle; wind vanes move
4–7 mph (6–11 kph)

3 GenTLe breeze
Leaves and twigs move
8–12 mph (12–19 kph)

4 ModeraTe breeze
Branches move; flags flap
13–18 mph (20–29 kph)

5 Fresh breeze
Small trees sway;
white caps on water
19–24 mph (30–39 kph)

6 STrong breeze
Large branches move; flags beat
25–31 mph (40–50 kph)

7 ModeraTe gaLe
Whole trees move;
flags extend
32–38 mph (51–61 kph)

8 Fresh gaLe
Twigs break;
walking is difficult
39–46 mph (62–74 kph)

9 STrong gaLe
Signs, antennae blow down
47–54 mph (76–87 kph)

10 WhoLe gaLe
Trees uproot
55–63 mph (88–102 kph)

11 STorm
Much general damage
64–73 mph (103–116 kph)

12 Hurricane
Widespread destruction
74+ mph (over 116 kph)

Make a Beaufort Scale Spinner

To estimate how hard the wind is blowing, observe its effects and match them up on this spinning Beaufort Scale!

HERE'S WHAT YOU NEED:

- **Fine-tipped marker**
- **Small plate**
- **2 sheets heavyweight paper**
- **Ruler**
- **Scissors**
- **Paper fastener**

HERE'S WHAT YOU DO:

1 Trace around the plate to make a circle on one of the sheets of paper. Divide the circle into 12 segments, using the ruler to draw straight lines.

2 Number the segments from 1 to 12. (Note: 0 and 1 are on one segment.) Referring to the Beaufort Scale chart, make a simple drawing on the widest part of each segment to illustrate the wind speed. Under each drawing, write a brief description and the wind speed in miles (or kilometers) per hour. Cut out the circle.

3 Cut out a smaller circle from the other sheet of paper. Cut a V shape, the same size as one of the segments of the larger circle, taking care to end the cuts before you reach the very center of the circle. Position this circle on top of the larger circle, and join with a paper fastener.

BE A METEOROLOGIST

MEASURE THE WIND SPEED

Measure the wind speed at different times of day and in different locations and record it in your log. What kind of relationship do you notice between location and wind speed?

WEATHER LORE

Can you use what you know about weather to come up with a meteorological explanation for each verse of this American folk poem? (Hint: Use your wind chart on page 46 for help.)

(1) When the wind is from the north,
The skillful fisherman goes not forth.

(2) When the wind is in the east,
That's when the fishing is the least.

(3) When the wind is in the south,
It blows flies in the fish's mouth.

(4) But when the wind is in the west,
That's when the fishing is the best.

ANSWERS! 1. Because north winds are cold, the fish and the flies are less active; so the fish aren't feeding as much.

2. Winds from the east signal a stormy day. Fewer flies and raw, cool, rainy weather mean the fish will be less active.

3. Warm winds from the south mean the fish will be busier, but there will be more natural food like flies, so catching them may be tricky.

4. West winds are dry and bring sunny weather, and in the warm weather months the temperatures will keep the fish active, making it great weather for fishing.

I was freezing while I was sledding this afternoon, but when I looked at the thermometer, the temperature wasn't all that cold. Why did I feel so cold?

You were probably feeling the wind chill! A nice cool breeze feels great on a hot day, but wind can be dangerous when it makes the temperature shown on the thermometer feel much colder. This effect is called the *wind chill factor*. When the wind blows and the temperature is cold, you need to bundle up even more to protect yourself.

The U.S. National Weather Service has devised the chart on the next page to help determine wind chill. Find the temperature across the top line and the speed of the wind in the left-hand column. Where the lines meet is the temperature that it will feel like to you, because of the wind chill factor.

WIND CHILL

Temperature (°Fahrenheit)

Wind Speed (mph)

	35°	30°	25°	20°	15°	10°	5°	0°	-5°	-10°	-15°	-20°	-25°	-30°
5	32	27	22	16	11	6	0	-5	-10	-15	-21	-26	-31	-36
10	22	16	10	3	-3	-9	-15	-22	-27	-34	-40	-46	-52	-58
15	16	9	2	-5	-11	-18	-25	-31	-38	-45	-51	-58	-65	-72
20	12	4	-3	-10	-17	-24	-31	-39	-46	-53	-60	-67	-74	-81
25	8	1	-7	-15	-22	-29	-36	-44	-51	-59	-66	-74	-81	-88
30	6	-2	-10	-18	-25	-33	-41	-49	-56	-64	-71	-79	-86	-93
35	4	-4	-12	-20	-27	-35	-43	-52	-58	-67	-74	-82	-89	-97

To convert Fahrenheit (°F) temperatures to Celsius (°C), see page 35.

To convert miles to kilometers, multiply the speed (mph) by 1.6.

QUICK-TAKE FORECASTS

Your thermometer reads 15° F (-9°C). Wearing your winter jacket, you start to head for the bus stop, but then you notice the large branches of an oak tree moving in the wind (see the Beaufort Scale, page 54). What is the wind chill? How should you dress?

ANSWER! The wind speed is 25 to 31 mph (40 to 50 kph), making the wind chill -22°F to -25°F (-30°C to -32°C). Better wear some extra layers under your jacket, and—very important—protect any exposed skin with a hat, scarf, and mittens!

The **windiest location** on earth is 6,288 feet (1,934 m) up in the air—on top of Mount Washington in New Hampshire. The buildings on the top of the mountain are either built into the rocks or are chained down so they won't blow away!

On April 12, 1934, the winds roared at 188 mph (302 kph) for 5 minutes, and then gusted to 231 mph (372 kph), still **the most powerful wind** that scientists have ever measured on the surface of the earth! The strongest winds of a hurricane (see page 106) have been measured at 200 mph (322 kph).

Where are the hardest places to forecast?

That would be near mountains. Weather changes dramatically near the mountains, sometimes in just a few hundred feet, which is a big challenge for forecasters. Mountains get stronger winds and bigger changes in temperature. Air gets cooler as it travels over mountains, making more clouds, rain, and snow there. Sinking air from the mountains warms up, creating heat waves in the summer and bringing sudden thaws in winter.

A Tight Squeeze

Why is Mount Washington so windy? As wind moves along, it meets obstacles (like buildings) and geographical features (deserts, mountains, or bodies of water) that can make it change speed or direction. Traveling past a tree, for example, causes the wind to slow down because it uses up some of its energy moving the leaves and branches.

When wind is forced over a mountain, the winds from the base of the mountain all the way to the top are squeezed through a much smaller space just above the mountain. Why doesn't the air above the mountain make room? The wind is moving that air along also, and it creates a barrier that only flexes a little. Getting all that air through the smaller spot above the mountain (with more air rushing in behind) means the wind must go faster to get through.

Try It: See how obstacles in your own yard or on the school playground affect wind speed. Use your anemometer to measure the wind at various locations. Take a reading in the middle of a clear open place on the ground. Next, measure the wind next to a garage, tree, or parked car. Take several readings at various heights. Record your observations in your log and compare them. How do the height and size of the obstacle affect the wind speed?

WATER
Completes The Mix

Warm weather, cold weather; hot, sunny beach days and crisp kite-flying days—what's missing in our weather mix? **Water!**

We have **precipitation** in the forms of rain, snow, sleet, and hail, because water is in the air.

Once you understand the effect of **air temperature** on that **water**, your forecasts will go a long way toward helping people understand how the weather affects their **comfort level**, whether they're bundling up against the sleet and snow, or trying to keep cool on a sticky summer day.

Disappearing Puddle Act

After it rains, find a puddle on your driveway or the sidewalk (or grab the hose and make one). Trace around it with chalk. Record the time of day and what the weather is like in your Weather Log. Come back several times and trace around it, each time in a different color. What happens by the end of the day (if it doesn't start raining again)?

No more puddle! The water in your puddle **evaporated**. This means it changed from liquid water to a gas, called **water vapor**. The warmer and drier the air, the faster the water disappears. Remember what happens to warm, light air (see page 23)? As the water vapor joins the warm, light air, it floats upward to mix with the other gases in the atmosphere.

WEATHER WORDS

Any kind of water falling from the sky—rain, snow, drizzle, hail—is called **precipitation**.

Making a Hair Hygrometer

Measure the humidity using a strand of your hair!

HERE'S WHAT YOU NEED:

- **Waterproof glue**
- **5 Popsicle sticks**
- **Strand of your hair**
- **Soapy cloth**
- **Waterproof markers**

HERE'S WHAT YOU DO:

1 Glue four of the sticks to each other in a row. Then, glue the fifth stick at the top so it forms a T.

2 Gently wipe off the strand of hair with the cloth. Glue one end of the hair to the horizontal stick. Mark the length of your hair on the vertical sticks.

3 Head outside with your hygrometer and stick it into the ground in a spot where it won't get knocked over (put rocks around the base if you need to).

To measure the amount of water vapor in the air, called **humidity**, meteorologists use a **hygrometer**.

BE A **METEOROLOGIST**

It's just a guess... but **I** think it's very humid in here.

HOW HUMID IS IT?

Every day, examine the hair on your hygrometer (holding a sheet of paper behind the hair makes it easier to see). How does the strand look when the weather is warm and dry? How does it change when it rains? Does the air feel different to you when the strand changes? What relationship do you observe between strand length and the general weather? (See how important the relationship between general observations and scientific observations is in forecasting?)

Hair soaks up the water vapor in the air, so a **humid** day (more vapor) sure can change your hairstyle! Some people end up with a slicked-down straight look as their strands of hair respond to all that moisture by getting longer, while other people's hair "expands" so that they turn into curlyheads or frizz-tops.

My hair hygrometer only showed me whether the air was dry or humid. Can I measure how much water is actually in the air?

Sure you can! But to measure the humidity you'll need another kind of hygrometer called a *psychrometer*.

Meteorologists compare the amount of moisture in the air to the total amount of moisture that the air could possibly hold at that same temperature. They express this comparison as a percentage called the relative humidity.

Remember, percent means "in every hundred," so when the air has a relative humidity of 50 percent, it is holding 50 out of a possible 100 parts of water vapor at that temperature. If the relative humidity is 100 percent, the air is holding 100 parts of water out of a possible 100 parts, so it can't absorb any more. Warm air can hold more moisture than cool air, so when the air temperature changes, the relative humidity changes.

"DEW" YOU KNOW WHERE THAT WATER CAME FROM?

You've probably already felt the effects of a change in the relative humidity—what happens to your sneakers when you walk across the grass early on a summer morning? They get soaked!

During the night, the air temperature just above the ground cools down. If the temperature gets so cool that the relative humidity is at or close to 100 percent, then the water vapor (a gas) begins to *condense* (turn back to liquid). These little droplets of water collect as *dew* on exposed surfaces like the grass. The temperature at which the water starts condensing is called the *dewpoint*.

If the air temperature near the ground is below

freezing (32°F/0°C) when the dewpoint is reached, the water vapor turns to ice instead of water droplets. We call that moisture *frost*!

WEATHER LORE

Dew on the grass, Rain will never pass.

This saying is a keeper! Dew can only form if there's no wind and few clouds. A heavy cloud cover would keep the heat from rising into the atmosphere, so the air couldn't cool to its dewpoint temperature. Wind would blow air over the ground, also preventing dew from forming. The calm, clear skies that allow dew to form also mean good weather, so morning dew does signal that conditions are right for a pleasant day.

Make a Psychrometer

Use this psychrometer to determine the relative humidity of the air.

HERE'S WHAT YOU NEED:

- **Scissors**
- **Empty cardboard milk or juice carton (64 ounces or 2 L)**
- **Glue**
- **2 thermometers (°F or °C)**
- **Shoelace or gauze**

HERE'S WHAT YOU DO:

1 Cut out a rectangle from the front of the carton at the bottom. Glue the thermometers to the carton so the bulbs are in front of the hole.

2 Soak the shoelace in water; then wrap it around the bulb of one thermometer.

The *dry-bulb thermometer* records the air temperature.

The thermometer wrapped in the wet gauze is *your wet-bulb thermometer*. As the water in the shoelace evaporates, the temperature of this thermometer will drop.

USING YOUR PSYCHROMETER

Set up the psychrometer on a table, and let a small fan blow on it until the temperatures stop falling. Record the temperature of each thermometer in your Weather Log. Then, subtract the temperature of the wet-bulb thermometer from that of the dry-bulb one.

    Using charts on pages 134 or 135, find the air temperature (the dry-bulb temperature) in the column on the left and the difference between the two temperatures in the row along the top. The number where the row and column intersect is the relative humidity.

Try It: Let's say the room you're in is 58°F (14°C) (the temperature of the dry-bulb thermometer) and the wet-bulb temperature is 50°F (10°C). Find 58° in the column on the left of the Fahrenheit chart (14°C on the Celsius chart) and 8°F (4°C) in the row across the top. The relative humidity in the room is 56 percent—the air is holding a little more than half the water that it can hold at 58°F (14°C).

Now, let's say the air in the room warms up to 68°F (20°C) while the amount of water vapor stays the same. You check your wet-bulb temperature and it has risen to 53°F (12°C), so the difference between the dry and wet bulbs has increased to 15°F (8°C). What happens to the relative humidity?

RELATIVE HUMIDITY IN °CELSIUS

Where the columns are blank, the relative humidity is zero (or very close). When you have a very large difference between the dry- and wet-bulb temperatures, relative humidity is so small that y measure it (less than one percent).

Difference between dry- and wet-bulb Tempera

°C	1	2	3	4	5	6	7	8	9
4	85	70	56	42	27	14			
5	85	71	58	44	31	18	5		
6	86	72	59	46	35	22	10		
7	86	73	60	48	37	25	14	3	
8	87	74	62	51	39	28	17	6	
9	87	75	63	53	41	31	20	10	
10	88	77	66	55	44	34	24	15	
11	89	78	67	56	46	36	27	18	
12	89	78	68	58	48	39	29		
	89	79	69	59	50	41			
			70	60	5				

ANSWER! The relative humidity drops to 34 percent [the intersection of 68°F on the left and 15°F (68°-53°) at the top of the chart on page 130]. On the Celsius chart, 20° on the left and 8° (20°-12°) at the top give a relative humidity of 39 percent (the conversion and rounding off of the temperatures result in this slight difference between the Fahrenheit and Celsius percentages).

FORECASTER'S "GETTING IT RIGHT" RULES!

- *As the air temperature rises, the amount of moisture in the air gets further away from the maximum amount the air can hold—and the relative humidity (percent of water vapor in the air) goes down.*

- *As the air temperature falls, the amount of moisture in the air gets closer to the maximum amount the air could hold—and the relative humidity goes up.*

WARMER

COOLER

Because warm air can hold more water than cold air, meteorologists like to measure the humidity of the air as a percentage of the amount of water that the air can hold at a given temperature. This measure is called the relative humidity.

ASK MARK!

Wait a minute! When I look at the charts, as the air temperature rises in the far left column, the relative humidity is also increasing. Didn't you just say the opposite?

You have sharp eyes—just what a weather forecaster needs! You're right—the chart does show the relative humidity rising as the air gets warmer. Higher temperatures have higher humidity to *start* with, because the warmer air can hold more water vapor in the first place. But the *"Getting-It-Right" Rules!* still hold! Let's go back to the example: If you had started at 68°F (instead of 58°F), the wet-bulb temperature would have been higher to start with, and you would have started with a higher relative humidity (greater than 51 percent). If the air had then warmed to 70°F, the difference between the wet- and dry-bulb temperatures would increase, and the relative humidity would *drop*. Air temperature *up*, relative humidity *down*—just like the rule says!

Relative humidity is a tricky concept—a lot of grownups I explain it to have a hard time understanding it! You'll get more comfortable with it as you use it more—and who knows, you may be explaining it to grownups before too long!

FORECASTER'S "GETTING IT RIGHT" RULES!

• The relative humidity of the air changes, depending on the air temperature.

• Cool air can't hold as much moisture as warm air, so as the temperaure drops, the moisture in the air gets closer to the maximum amount it can hold.

• Air eventually cools to a point where it can't hold any more moisture (100 percent relative humidity) and has to start letting go of it, so dew forms.

WEATHER LORE

Try your hand at a meteorological explanation for this weather saying. Then, see how yours compares with the "official" one below.

If Mrs. Spider hangs her wash on the Line,
The weather will be fine.

But today is **NOT** laundry day!

ANSWER! "Wash on the line" is a poetic way of noticing the dew drops clinging to the intricate lines of a spider's web. And you know what dew in the morning means (see page 69)!

BE A
METEOROLOGIST

MEASURE THE HUMIDITY

Determine the relative humidity for one week and record it in your Weather Log. Observe the temperature and how sticky or dry it feels. Are storms more likely to happen on a dry day or a humid day? How does the weather feel on a cool day when the humidity is high, as opposed to a warm day?

QUICK-TAKE ? FORECASTS

The relative humidity is 40 percent when dark clouds arrive and a cool rain begins, causing the temperature to fall. What happens to the relative humidity?

ANSWER! **It goes up.** The cooler air can't hold as much water vapor as the warmer air, so the moisture in the air gets closer to the maximum amount possible, raising the relative humidity.

On a hot day, have you ever heard someone say "It's not the heat; it's the humidity that's making me so uncomfortable!" The amount of water vapor in the air affects how efficiently your body can release heat and cool you off. When there is less water vapor in the air, your sweat can evaporate (see page 65) from your skin. But if there is a lot of water vapor already in the air, your sweat doesn't have anywhere to go, so it just sits there, making you feel sticky—and even hotter.

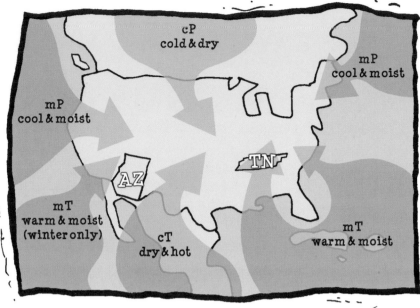

Why does a summer day with a temperature of 90°F (32°C) feel so much hotter in Tennessee than it does in Arizona?

The air in Arizona (AZ) is very dry, so a summer day feels hot but tolerable. A summer day in Tennessee (TN), however, forces people into air-conditioned buildings for relief. In the southeastern United States, where warm, moist air arrives from the tropics, the air is very humid, slowing the evaporation of perspiration from your skin and making you feel hot and sweaty.

A 90°F (32°C) day in Arizona would typically have a wet-bulb temperature of 70°F (21°C), which gives us a relative humidity of 36 percent. A 90°F day in Tennessee, however, would most often have a wet-bulb temperature of 80°F (27°C). Figure out the relative humidity. How do the relative humidities compare?

C = continental, or air masses formed over land

m = maritime, or air masses formed over oceans

P = Polar

T = Tropical

ANSWER! The relative humidity (see pages 134–135) in Tennessee would be 65 percent. Whew! Crank up the air conditioner!

CLouds
The Key To Weather Forecasting

What happens to all that warm, light **water vapor** rising up into the atmosphere? A lot of it turns into **clouds!** Meteorologists keep a very close eye on clouds: their size, shape, and where they hang out in the sky tell forecasters what weather those clouds will bring.

So, learn to "read" the clouds and you'll amaze your friends and family with your **weather predictions!**

There's a Cloud in The Kitchen!

Boil some water in a pan with a grownup's help. Hold a cool metal lid over the pan. What happens to the water vapor when it hits the lid?

As water vapor rises up into the cooler layers of the upper atmosphere, it cools down. You already know what happens to water vapor when it cools off (remember your wet sneakers?). It condenses (see page 69), just the way it does in the kitchen when it hits the cool metal lid.

Clouds are floating collections of condensed water droplets (or ice crystals, when the clouds form higher up in the atmosphere where it's colder). You've probably been inside a cloud before and didn't even know it! Fog is simply a cloud near the ground.

NEWMAN!

MEOW!

A Day in the Life of a Raindrop

See if you can trick your friends with this weather question:

What does every raindrop start off as?

Did they answer **"A snowflake"**? They're right! Almost every raindrop, even on a hot summer day, begins its life as a snowflake!

High up where most clouds form, the temperature is below freezing (32°F/0°C), so the water vapor turns to ice. The ice collects on tiny particles of soot, pollen, dust, and pollution, creating snow crystals that grow until they are heavy enough to begin their trip toward the ground.

- If the air is below freezing all the way from the cloud to the ground, then the snowflakes stay snowflakes.

- If the air near the ground is above freezing, the snowflakes melt, forming softer, wetter snowflakes or changing to raindrops.

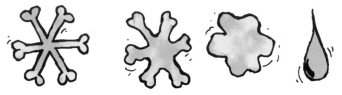

- Sometimes the warm and cold air is in layers, so the snowflakes melt, refreeze, melt, refreeze—you get the idea.

- If there is a very thick layer of cold air near the ground, the raindrops slow down and freeze into tiny ice pellets, or *sleet*, bouncing on the ground and rattling windowpanes—and stinging your cheeks!

- If there is only a thin layer of cold air near the ground (just a few hundred yards/meters), then the raindrops don't have time to freeze. But if the temperature of what they land on is below freezing, they freeze as soon as they touch it.

  Freezing rain is one of the most dangerous types of precipitation because the ice weighs down power lines and tree limbs and makes travel extremely difficult (not to mention the coating of ice over steps, pathways—you name it!).

Try It: Place a softball-sized rock in your freezer for a few days. Wearing gloves, take the rock out and sprinkle it lightly with cold water. What forms on the rock?

 **ANSWER!** **Freezing Rain!**

WEATHER WATCHERS

"Snowflake" Bentley

Wilson A. "Snowflake" Bentley was a Vermont farmer with a passion for snowflakes. He decided, at age 16, to devote his life to photographing them. After capturing and photographing more than 6,000 of these delicate crystals, he concluded that no two snowflakes are exactly alike!

How can you tell where rain is falling?

Here's a meteorologist's tip: As dark clouds approach, watch for the color to lighten up just a little. Raindrops reflect light, making the clouds a little brighter, so that's where it will be raining.

As Light as a feather...

What weighs 10 million pounds (4,500,000 kg) but can float in the air? Believe it or not, it's a cloud!

Why don't clouds fall out of the sky? Well, they try! Gravity is always slowly pulling the clouds down but the rising air that makes clouds pushes them back up! Even if clouds could keep falling, they'd evaporate long before they fell on you!

...not!

Make a Rain Gauge

A wide-mouth jar works best for collecting rainfall. Then, use a narrower jar to make the rain gauge, so you can precisely measure even very small amounts of rain.

HERE'S WHAT YOU NEED:

- **Ruler**
- **Wide-mouth collecting jar**
- **Straight-sided clear jar about 1" to 1½" (2.5 to 3 cm) in diameter for gauge**
- **Permanent marker**

Measuring jar   Collecting jar

HERE'S WHAT YOU DO:

Set the ruler in your collecting jar and fill it with 1" (2.5 cm) of water. Pour the water into the narrow jar. Label the level of the water as 1" (2.5 cm) and then divide that into smaller increments, such as ⅛", ¼", and ½" (2.5 mm, 5 mm, and 1 cm).

MEASURING RAINFALL

Set your collecting jar in an open area. Measure the amount of rain in your rain gauge every day (then empty it) and record your measurements for a period of a week or two. (You may have to leave your jar out longer to have a measurable amount of precipitation, depending on the time of year and the seasonal rainfall patterns where you live.)

When do you get more rain—when it falls slowly and steadily or when it's a short but heavy downpour?

What kind of high-tech gadget does a meteorologist use to measure rainfall?

Well, actually, it's not high tech! What we use is similar to your rain gauge. The standard rain gauge the United States National Weather Service uses is a metal cylinder, 10" (40 cm) across, mounted 4' (1.5 m) above the ground (so that water hitting the ground doesn't splash into the gauge).

Different countries use rain gauges of different sizes, so it is difficult to make accurate international comparisons of rainfall amounts.

WEATHER RECORDS

The **wettest** place in the world is Mount Waialeale, on the island of Kauai in Hawaii. It gets about 460 inches (1,150 cm) of rain every year. That's more than 38 feet (11.7 m)!

But if it's **thunderstorms** you're looking for, head for the island of Java in Indonesia. It has thunderstorms about 322 days a year!

CLOUDS: BIG CLUES FOR WEATHER FORECASTERS

The two most important things to observe about a cloud are

- iTs shape
- how high iT is in The sky

Learn to "read" these "signs," and you'll really amaze your friends and family with your weather predictions!

Did you bring an umbrella?

Luke Howard

Luke Howard was an amateur meteorologist. In 1803, he created a cloud identification system that classified clouds by their shapes and heights. He named 10 categories of clouds, all stemming from the three major types: cirrus, cumulus, and stratus.

THE LEGION OF CLOUD HEROES

These guys will help you remember the Latin meanings of clouds' names, the key to clouds' shapes and where they hang out in the sky!

ALTO MAN	THE INCREDIBLE CIRRUS	QUEEN CUMULUS	NIMBUS THE WHINER	STRATUS BOY
alto = high	cirrus = curl	cumulus = pile	nimbus = rain	stratus = layer

A Key for Cloudwatchers

Heights are approximate; Cumulonimbus can reach 70,000 ft (22,000m)

SST
(50,000 ft/15,800 m)

Commercial jetliner
(35,000 ft/11,000 m)

Cirrus

Cirrostratus

Anvil Cloud
(Top of Cumulonimbus)

Cirrocumulus

Breitling Orbiter 3
Round-the-world balloon
(33,000 ft/10,400 m)

10 miles
(52,800 ft/16,700 m)

9 miles
(47,520 ft/15,000 m)

8 miles
(42,240 ft/13,300 m)

7 miles
(36,960 ft/11,600 m)

6 miles
(31,680 ft/10,000 m)

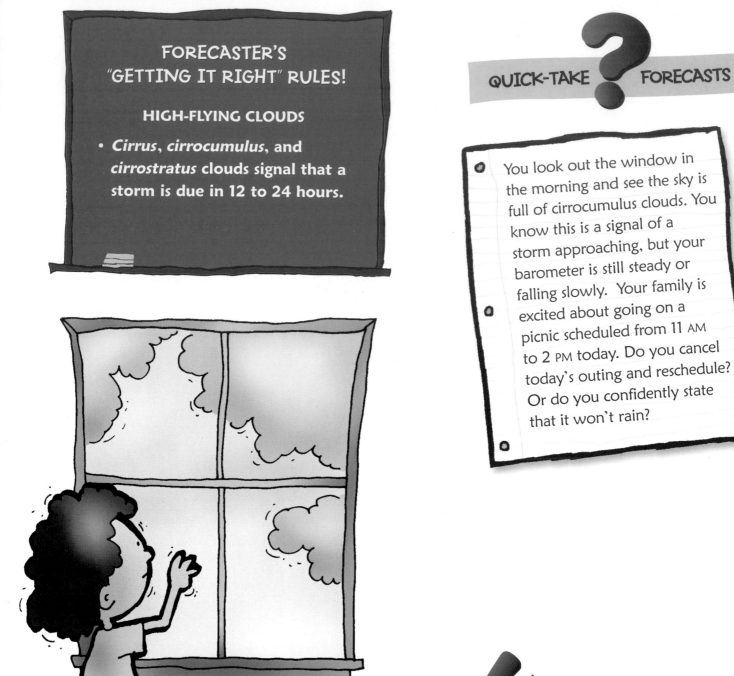

FORECASTER'S "GETTING IT RIGHT" RULES!

HIGH-FLYING CLOUDS

- *Cirrus*, *cirrocumulus*, and *cirrostratus* clouds signal that a storm is due in 12 to 24 hours.

QUICK-TAKE ? FORECASTS

You look out the window in the morning and see the sky is full of cirrocumulus clouds. You know this is a signal of a storm approaching, but your barometer is still steady or falling slowly. Your family is excited about going on a picnic scheduled from 11 AM to 2 PM today. Do you cancel today's outing and reschedule? Or do you confidently state that it won't rain?

ANSWER! Although those cirrocumulus clouds will continue to arrive and make the afternoon cloudier, you've checked your barometer so you can assure everyone that it won't rain during the picnic. Your family can go ahead with its plans.

FORECASTER'S "GETTING IT RIGHT" RULES!

STUCK-IN-THE-MIDDLE CLOUDS

- When *altostratus* clouds show up by themselves, they usually just mean some light precipitation will fall here and there.

- When *cirrus* clouds are dropping to alto-type clouds, look for rain or snow in less than 12 hours.

Your new sled has been collecting dust, and you are anxious for snow. After some sunshine this morning, altostratus clouds showed up quickly. The barometer is falling a bit, and the wind is from the southwest. Is this the storm that dumps the snow?

ANSWER! Not likely. Showing up suddenly, altostratus clouds might be just a weak weather system that brings light precipitation instead of part of a bigger storm. Also, winds from the southwest are mild and dry, which could limit the amount of moisture for the storm. Your sled may have to wait a little longer.

FORECASTER'S "GETTING IT RIGHT" RULES!

"HOW-LOW-CAN-YOU-GO?" CLOUDS

- *Cumulus* clouds are fair-weather clouds; you'll see these big, white clouds when the sky is a clear blue.

- *Stratus* clouds will linger, perhaps with a little drizzle, until the wind, the temperature, or the barometer begins to change.

- *Stratocumulus* clouds mean sprinkles, except near mountains where rain or snow are more likely.

- Low, flat *nimbostratus* clouds are already in the process of raining or snowing, which doesn't leave much room for prediction—except that the precipitation will eventually end!

QUICK-TAKE ? FORECASTS

You've been waiting to go outside all morning, but nimbostratus clouds have been bringing rain. The clouds won't give you many clues, so what clues in the wind or the barometer would help you forecast when the rain will end?

ANSWER! Winds shifting so they're out of the west, bringing in drier air, usually signal the end of the rain within a few hours. A barometer rising indicates the storm, with its lower pressure, is moving away, and rain should lighten up and end within a few hours. If the wind direction is still northeast to south, and the pressure is falling, rain (or snow) will last several more hours.

BE A
METEOROLOGIST

READ THE CLOUDS!

Look up at the sky today. Can you identify any of the clouds? For the next week, observe the clouds and the weather they bring, recording your observations in your Weather Log.

Then, use your newfound cloud-weather pattern awareness to predict what weather is on the way, based on the cloud formations. Write your forecast down in your log, and compare your prediction to the actual weather. Are your forecasts improving?

WATCH OUT for...

Here's a cloud to keep a close eye on! Starting in the lower part of the atmosphere as a cumulus cloud, it grows larger and taller until its top is flattened by strong winds. This huge, dark, threatening-looking thundercloud is called *cumulonimbus*, a sign that a thunderstorm (see page 97) is approaching.

...cumulonimbus!

WEATHER LORE

Ring around The sun or moon,
Rain or snow is coming soon.

Remember this handy saying! It looks as if there is a big ring of light around the sun or the moon, called a **halo**, when sunlight passes through all the ice crystals in a cirrostratus cloud. And we all know what those clouds mean—stormy weather is on the way.

Create Your Own Weather Saying

Look back through all the information you've gathered in your Weather Log. Consider all the weather forecasting clues you know so far, such as temperature, what happens when the air pressure or humidity changes, and the kind of cloud you see. Make up a saying to help you remember what certain weather conditions mean.

HERE'S ONE TO GET YOU STARTED:

If The wind is a-whippin'
and iT's gray up There,
A sTorm may be a-comin',
so you'd beTTer Take care!

NOW, IT'S YOUR TURN!

Why do gardeners in cool climates cover their crops with blankets in the fall when they see a bright or full moon at night?

Some gardeners believe that the full moon will bring cold air, which could damage their plants. The truth is there is nothing about the moon that causes the temperatures to drop. However, the belief isn't entirely wrong: if you can see the moon, it means the sky is clear and cloudless.

Without cloud cover, any heat from the earth is free to go out into space, lowering the air temperature, so that water vapor in the air turns to frost. The clear skies, not the moon, mean a higher chance of frost. Now, make that into a weather saying!

Weather on The Wild Side

Do you think predicting the weather ever gets to be a ho-hum routine for weather forecasters? Not with **storms** around!

Believe it or not, storms actually **calm** the weather down—they're **nature's way** of bringing back the peace and quiet—but they certainly can be destructive too.

When the weather threatens to get **wild**, people need time to **prepare** for dangerous weather conditions, so they really depend on weather forecasters for accurate information.

GUESS THE MOST COMMON STORM ON EARTH!

HINT: There are an average of 50,000 of them all over the world every day, adding up to 10 million lightning strikes a day! That's right, thunder-and-lightning storms are the most common "wild weather" situations!

Lightning and thunder are quite a team. Lightning is flashy and steals the spotlight, but a clap of thunder makes you sit up and pay attention. As air currents and cloud droplets bounce up and down inside a thundercloud (see page 89), static electricity builds up. (You've probably felt static electricity before, when you shuffle across a carpet and then touch something—zap!) This same kind of static electricity is released as a very hot flash of light, and we see a bolt of lightning. The heat causes the air to expand so rapidly that it creates a sound just like an explosion. A thunderclap!

THE CHALLENGER

Have you ever had an airplane flight delayed or canceled because of bad weather? Weather affects space travel too. Lightning is a serious threat: there can be no lightning within 11.5 miles (19 km) 30 minutes prior to launch for a space shuttle launch to go ahead.

It wasn't lightning, however, that led to the space shuttle *Challenger* disaster in January 1986. Partly because of cold weather and buffeting winds during the launch, a faulty rubber sealing ring resulted in a small gas leak. When the shuttle was launched, the fuel supply ignited in one enormous explosion.

All of the astronauts on board were killed. Among them was elementary school teacher Christa McAuliffe, the first civilian selected to go into space.

In 1752, Benjamin Franklin decided to fly his kite in a thunderstorm (definitely not a good thing for you to try!)—and the rest is history! To see if he could capture electrical energy from the storm, Franklin tied a key to the kite string. As lightning flashed, sure enough, the wet string carried electricity down to the key and sparks jumped!

HOW FAR AWAY IS THE STORM?

Although lightning and thunder occur at the same instant, you see the flash before hearing the boom. Light travels fast, about 186,000 miles (299,274 km) per second, so you see it the instant it happens. But sound moves much more slowly, covering only about one mile every five seconds (1 km/3 seconds). The difference between these two speeds gives us a great way to estimate how far the lightning is from you.

Try It: As a bolt of lightning streaks across the sky, begin counting the seconds, "one thundercloud, two thunderclouds, three thunderclouds," and so on until you hear the thunder. If you count five seconds, the lightning is only one mile (1.6 km) away; if you count to 10 seconds, it is two miles (3.2 km) away, and so on.

You've been watching lightning and counting until you hear the thunder. After a few times of counting to only three or four, you notice the next time you make it to 10. Then you count to 15—how far away is the lightning now? Is the storm getting closer or moving away? Is it safe to go outside?

LIGHTNING SAFETY RULES!

TO STAY SAFE DURING A THUNDERSTORM:

- **Get indoors as soon as possible (if you're far from any buildings, the next best choice is a car).**

- **Don't stand in an open field or a boat or take shelter under a large tree that stands alone (lightning hits the tallest things first).**

- **Don't use any electrical appliances (that includes the cordless phone!).**

- **Don't swim (water conducts electricity).**

- **Remember, "If you can see it, if you can hear it, then flee it!"**

ANSWER! On a count of 15, the lightning is now three miles (4.8 km) away. The storm is moving away, but it is not gone. Wait at least 30 minutes after the last thunder to go back outside.

You are the head umpire at a championship softball game. Weather conditions have you wondering if you should postpone the game for safety's sake. Nobody likes to postpone games (and umps are already not the most popular people), so you want to make sure it's totally necessary to call off the game.

Which of these two situations would make it necessary to postpone the game?

1. Sweat has been sticking to your skin. Winds are blowing gently south to east and the barometer is falling. The clouds are puffy and reach high up into the sky.

2. Your cold can of lemonade is covered with beads of condensation. Winds are blowing at high speed east to north, and the barometer is falling. The clouds are puffy and reach high up into the sky. You see a streak of lightning, but when you counted, you determined it was 20 miles (32 km) away.

ANSWERS! Hot, humid weather can lead to thunderstorms, and winds from the south to east can bring storms. Plus, falling pressure and cumulus clouds are both signs of approaching storms. But in **#1** the winds are blowing gently, not quickly—so there's probably plenty of time to play the game.

In **#2**, high winds are blowing, the wind direction calls for rain, plus the barometer is falling. Most important, you have already seen a streak of lightning, and even though it is far away, you never want the players out on the field when there's lightning. Sorry, folks, the game is postponed!

PING-PONG IN THE CLOUDS

It seems odd to have balls of ice dropping out of the sky when it's not winter, but hailstorms occur during thunderstorm season—spring, summer, and fall. The tops of the huge thunderclouds reach way up into the atmosphere, where the temperature is below freezing. As raindrops fall, strong winds blow them up near the top of the thundercloud, where they freeze. Down they come again, getting coated with other raindrops along the way, and the winds push them back up, where they freeze into larger balls of ice. Up and down they bounce, growing larger and larger, until finally gravity pulls these hailstones down.

Try It: Slice open a hailstone, and you'll see a series of rings, like an onion. Count the rings and you'll know how many up-and-down trips through the thundercloud that hailstone took!

The **largest recorded hailstone** fell in Aurora, Nebraska, in 2003. It was 18¾ inches (47.6 cm) in circumference and weighed almost two pounds (907 g)!

TOO MUCH RAIN . . .

Floods cause more damage and take more lives than any other type of weather disaster. A flood happens when land that is normally dry is suddenly under water, because heavy rain has caused a body of water to rise so fast that it overflows. In severe floods, water can destroy entire towns and ruin huge areas of farmland.

. . . OR TOO LITTLE

A drought is a prolonged period of hot, dry weather with much less rain than normal. Plants, animals, (and sometimes people) die without enough water to drink. Farmers' crops fail, and this can lead to widespread hunger. Sometimes months or even years go by without sufficient rain.

WEATHER RECORDS

The **longest drought** was in Atacama, Chile. It lasted 400 years!

RECORDED IN HISTORY

THE DUST BOWL

The Dust Bowl was an area of the United States that included parts of Oklahoma, Texas, Colorado, New Mexico, and Kansas.

In the early 1900s, farmers plowed up the grasses that grew there naturally and planted wheat. Then, between 1934 and 1937, the region suffered a severe drought. Without water, the wheat didn't grow. Without the grass to hold it in place, the soil literally blew away, ruining farms from Texas all the way to Canada. The duststorms were so big you could see them from hundreds of miles (km) away, so you can see how this region got its nickname.

Eventually the federal government stepped in to replant grass and trees. Farmers learned the hard way how important those prairie grasses were and changed their farming methods.

HEAVY RAIN + COLD TEMPERATURES = SNOWSTORM!

Snow is such fun to play in— how could it be dangerous?

In snowy conditions, driving a car can be tricky, especially if there is a *whiteout*—where winds whip the snow around in the air so you can barely see in front of you. Sometimes the snow gets deep so quickly that even emergency vehicles get stuck! The weight of snow can cause roofs to collapse, and it can bring down tree branches and power lines.

When heavy snow combines with winds of at least 35 mph (56 kph) and temperatures are less than 20°F (-7°C), you've got a *blizzard*. A heavy snowstorm in the New England and Mid-Atlantic states in the United States is called a *nor'easter*: Northeast winds pick up lots of moisture as they move over the Atlantic Ocean, and the moisture becomes snow when it hits the East Coast and cools down.

WEATHER RECORDS

The most snow from one storm fell on Mount Shasta in California February 13–19, 1959— a whopping 189 inches (473 cm)!

Capture Those Weather Memories

Ask a grandparent or older friend to share some memories of "wild" weather. Maybe they survived the Blizzard of 1922, where it snowed 19 inches (48 cm) in Washington, D.C., a city not used to getting that much snow. Or perhaps they recall a time of drought when farmers they knew lost their crops, or when ads ran on the radio to "take a bath with a friend!"

Make a list of questions in your Weather Log so you'll be prepared. Ask your friend or relative how it affected them personally, and then how it affected their community and state or province. Be sure to ask about weather technology that was available at the time and how informed people were during the weather event. Are there any newspaper clippings about the event they could share with you?

Now, begin keeping photos and clippings from major weather events in *your* life to share 50 years from now!

WEATHER LORE

Have you ever noticed your cat or dog acting peculiarly right before a storm? Many believe that animals are more sensitive to changes in air pressure and can "sense" when a storm is approaching. In addition to pets acting nervously:

- Birds fly low because the insects they feed on are flying lower.

- Cows, horses, and sheep become restless and herd together.

- Frogs croak loudly and don't leave the water.

Tornado Touchdown

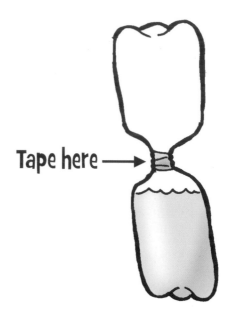

Tape here →

When thunderstorms reach their greatest strength, they sometimes create one of nature's most spectacular but destructive events—a tornado. The same strong rising air currents that make thunderstorms can create a spinning column of air inside the thundercloud. Most of these columns just spin until they die out, but if they touch the ground, that's when you've got a tornado, or a "twister."

A powerful tornado can have winds up to 300 miles per hour (483 kph). That's enough to blow a railroad car right off its track!

Try IT: Fill a two-liter plastic soda bottle with water and tape another bottle to it, opening to opening. Swirl the water; then, flip it so it drains into the bottle below. The spinning column you see in the water is a mini-tornado!

WEATHER RECORDS

More tornadoes happen in the United States than any other place on earth. Most strike during April and May in "Tornado Alley," an area from Texas and Oklahoma north to Kansas and Nebraska and east to Missouri. This huge, flat area is the perfect "meeting place" for different types of air that don't like to mix. Warm, wet air from the Gulf of Mexico collides with cold air from central Canada and dry air blowing in from the Rockies in the western United States, forming more than 700 tornadoes a year.

A tornado in early stages of formation, Oklahoma, May 1973

What was the worst weather event you ever had to forecast? How did you warn people?

I forecast in Vermont, where there are very few tornadoes or hurricanes. Winter weather is the most challenging, and it was never more dangerous than the January 1998 ice storm, one of the worst ice storms ever recorded in North America. Two to four inches (5 to 10 cm) of rain froze on every exposed surface in most of Maine and Quebec, and parts of Vermont, New Hampshire, and New York. Whole trees snapped in half, bringing down power lines. More than 100,000 people lost electricity, leaving them with no heat or lights for up to a week during the coldest time of the year.

The forecast information I provided to utility companies allowed them to move equipment before the roads were closed because of the ice. With their equipment in the right locations, they could restore power to people faster. And I was able to warn people about icy roads and suggest alternate routes that were still safe.

Be Prepared for Storms!

A tornado is approaching your town, and you have to think and act quickly. Where will you go? How will you keep your pets safe? What emergency supplies will you need? Do you have any possessions that are very valuable to you that you would want to take? Do you have elderly neighbors or relatives that you would want to check on?

Make a plan with your family for emergency weather situations. Discuss what to do in a weather disaster: how to get up-to-date weather information; where to store emergency supplies; and how to make sure that all family members will be safe. Put together a weather emergency kit: candles and dry matches, flashlights and extra batteries, a transistor radio, canned food with a manual or battery-operated can opener, and plenty of bottled water. No matter where you live, this emergency kit will come in very handy.

Better Stay Tuned!

Do you know the difference between a watch and a warning?

A *watch* is issued first. It reports there's a possibility for a storm or other potentially dangerous weather event (like a flood) to hit your area within a stated number of hours. Keep listening to emergency weather broadcasts for updates.

A *warning* is issued when the weather event has actually been spotted and will hit your neighborhood in a stated number of hours. Everyone should seek emergency shelter when a storm warning is issued and officials advise you to do so.

For emergency bulletins, check the Weather Channel or the National Oceanic and Atmospheric Administration's Weather Radio Stations (see page 137), or tune into a local radio station. In Canada, check the Meteorological Service of Canada's Weatheradio (see page 138).

When a bad weather event is heading your way, do you get called into work? Who takes care of your family?

If there is a serious weather situation, sometimes I need to stay longer at work or go in earlier. During Hurricane Floyd in September 1999, I went to work early. I had to use my chainsaw to cut through two fallen trees to get down the road, and then I had to read some of my weather information with a flashlight because the power was out at the office! (My family is very experienced with camping equipment and heating with a woodstove, so I feel confident they'll be comfortable and safe when I'm called in.)

I do get some weather information at home, so I could still forecast even if I couldn't get to my office, but this has never happened to me in 20 years of forecasting.

STORMS THAT START AT SEA

Sometimes a cluster of big thunderstorms, called a *tropical disturbance*, forms over warm ocean water. If the winds pick up speed to 40 mph (64 kph), it turns into a *tropical storm*.

Once winds reach 74 mph (119 kph), the tropical storm officially becomes a *hurricane*. Once the storm is over land, it starts to lose power but winds from storms over the ocean can push a lot of water up against the shore, causing coastal flooding. This *storm surge* is the most damaging part of a hurricane.

The storm surge of Hurricane Camille in August 1969 pushed these huge ships in Mississippi way up on shore.

FORECASTER'S "GETTING IT RIGHT" RULES!

Hurricanes are very difficult to predict, even for experts. But there are some things to keep in mind:

- **These are the necessary ingredients for a hurricane to form: warm ocean waters (at least 80°F/27°C), thunderstorms, and powerful winds.**

- **Florida and Texas, and south to Mexico and the Caribbean islands are struck by hurricanes coming from the east.**

- **In the Gulf of Mexico and on the East Coast, the storms almost always come from the south.**

- **Hurricanes may be very powerful, but they are also very fussy! They must have light winds *around* them, so as the darker storm clouds approach, winds will be light.**

You should never have the chance to try these rules, however, because the National Hurricane Center in Miami, Florida, helps local governments issue evacuation alerts before the storm arrives. *Follow their advice!*

In Canada, hurricanes are rare. But the eastern provinces can be affected, and residents can stay informed through the Canadian Hurricane Centre in Halifax, Nova Scotia.

QUICK-TAKE ? FORECASTS

The ocean temperature measures 77°F (25°C), it's almost noon, and you're feeling hot in your black T-shirt. The barometer is falling quickly, and you just heard the National Weather Service issue a hurricane watch. Winds are light, but you see dark clouds over the ocean. Should you go water skiing today?

ANSWER! **No.** The sea temperature is warm and the winds are light—weather hurricanes love. A hurricane watch means people along the coast may need to head to a safer place. Water skiing is out.

WEATHER LORE

Here's an old Florida saying to help you remember when the hurricane season occurs.

June, too soon,
July, stand by,
August, beware you must,
September, time to unlimber,
October, not over,
November, remember.

C-130 Hercules

Why did the U.S. National Weather Service start naming hurricanes?

Using names helped to clearly identify storms, which is very important to ships traveling the open ocean. If there is more than one storm, names like Hurricane Floyd and Hurricane Bob are much harder to confuse than numbers ("storm 1," "storm 2," etc).

Would you fly right into a...

Yes, if you were a Hurricane Hunter, part of the United States Air Force Reserve. These pilots are very brave—they fly their airplanes right into hurricanes and tropical storms. Their planes carry special weather sensors to gather critical information regarding a hurricane's strength and direction. The data is sent via satellite to the forecasters at the National Hurricane Center in Miami, Florida. Here, hurricane experts use the data to create an accurate picture of the storm so they can make a better forecast of what the storm is likely to do next.

...hurricane?

WEATHER WORDS

Hurricane comes from the West Indian word *huracan*, which means "big wind." A hurricane that occurs over the Pacific Ocean is called a **typhoon**, from the Chinese word *taifun*, or "great wind." So, a typhoon and a hurricane are the same thing—they're just called by different names in different parts of the world.

Typhoon damage to a coconut plantation in the Caroline Islands in the Pacific Ocean

Do we ever "over-forecast," causing people to evacuate and make emergency preparations for storms that never happen?

When weather forecasters issue watches and warnings, they are thinking about people's safety and how unpredictable the weather can sometimes be. If there is even a chance that a hurricane or a tornado will hit, or that a winter storm will cause heavy ice or snow, then it's important to warn people that conditions may become dangerous, giving them time to prepare.

And the early warnings have been successful. From 1916 to 1954, the average number of deaths from tornadoes in the United States was 225 people each year. Since 1955, the average has dropped to about 100. Meteorologists work very hard at making forecasts of severe weather more accurate.

BE A METEOROLOGIST

"THIS IS AN EMERGENCY BROADCAST"

There's a hurricane on the way, and people are tuning into the local weather station for information. What are the weather conditions? What should people do in their homes to stay safe? What supplies should they be sure to have on hand? Or should they evacuate?

Write a script to be broadcast over the local TV and radio stations to keep the residents of your town safe during this weather emergency!

Fine-Tuning Your Forecast

You're getting to be a pretty good forecaster! You know all about **humidity**, **wind**, **barometric pressure**, **temperature**, and **clouds**, and you've learned how to consider more and more weather variables when making your predictions. You even know the signs that a **major storm** is brewing and what to do in a weather emergency.

There are a few more tools that forecasters use to piece together the forecast puzzle. So let's sharpen your **forecasting skills** even more!

A ROAD MAP FOR THE WEATHER

Barometric highs and lows, temperature, precipitation, wind speed, and direction—whew! Fortunately for meteorologists, thousands of these weather measurements are put together into one big picture of what the weather is doing called a *weather map*.

Local weather stations across the United States report their conditions to the National Centers for Environmental Prediction (NCEP). This information is used to create national weather maps. From them, meteorologists can get a picture of weather patterns at a glance and use this information to create local weather maps for their areas and to make their forecasts. In Canada, weather information is collected and reported by the Meteorological Service of Canada.

Here's what this weather map tells us: With all those high-pressure systems (H), it's a pretty nice day in most of the United States! In the Midwest, however, low pressure (L), a cold front, and thicker clouds mean rainy, stormy weather there. But high pressure in southern Canada is clearing the skies behind that cold front.

WEATHER WORDS

The first places meteorologists look for action on the weather map are **fronts**. Warm and cold air don't like to mix. Where masses of cold, dry air run into warm, moist air, you can count on a struggle for control. Along this narrow meeting zone, called a front, temperature, wind, and moisture change rapidly.

PUSHY AIR UP FRONT, PLEASE!

Weather fronts are named for the type of air that is taking over—or winning the struggle for control.

A *cold front* forms when cold air wedges under warm air and pushes it up. The warm air cools quickly. You've seen what happens to the moisture in warm air when it cools. Clouds and short bursts of heavy precipitation form, and thunderstorms are typical.

A *warm front* forms when the warm air pushes its way up and over the cold air. As it gently rises, it cools gradually. A warm front causes steadier, more widespread precipitation that lasts for several hours.

A *stationary front* is just what the name says—"stay-tionary" means "stays in one place." Warm air still runs up and over the colder air, like a warm front, but the warm and cold air are mostly traveling sideways along the front. Some stationary fronts are very quiet, while others cause rain to fall over the same area for extended periods of time, a situation forecasters watch carefully because too much rain can cause flooding.

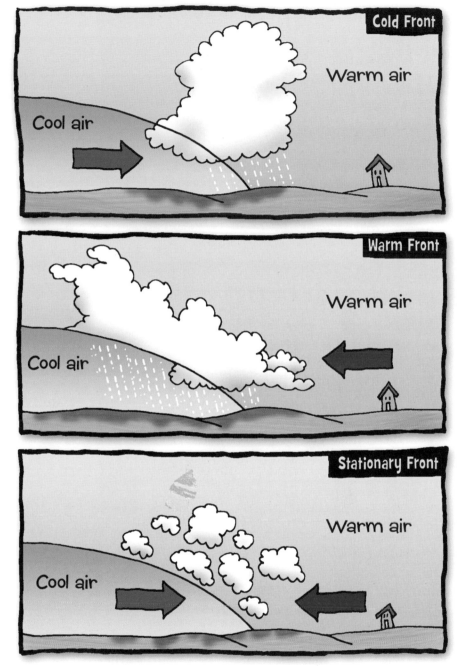

FORECASTER'S "GETTING IT RIGHT" RULES!

- Your barometer will drop as a front approaches and rise as it moves by (because warm air is rising, then cooling).

- A *cold front* causes briefer but harder precipitation.

- A *warm front* causes steadier, longerlasting precipitation.

- *Warm fronts mark the beginning of a storm.* Storms generally travel from west to east, so winds before the storms are moving air along from a warmer, southerly direction.

- *Cold fronts mark the end of a storm.* As the storm passes, winds change to the north and west, bringing colder air along.

QUICK-TAKE ? FORECASTS

A cold front has been spotted 300 miles (483 km) to the west of you. Your barometer shows the air pressure is dropping quickly. Wind speed is 21 mph (34 kph), blowing south to southeast. You are hosting a family reunion barbecue in three days. Should you reserve a big tent to cover the picnic tables?

ANSWER! It's a tough call. Rain is likely with the pressure dropping, brisk winds blowing south to southeast, and a cold front already spotted to the west. But cold fronts move through quickly and wind speed is already 21 mph (34 kph), meaning the storm could pass through before your party and conditions could clear up in plenty of time. Better safe than sorry, though. Rent the tent (and hope that the wind doesn't blow it away!).

BE A
METEOROLOGIST

READING A WEATHER MAP

There are simplified versions of weather maps that appear on TV during the forecast on the evening news, on the weather channels, and in the newspaper. Check one out! You'll be amazed at all the weather information you already know

how to interpret once you understand the symbols.

Listen to the next-day forecast and make notes in your Weather Log. Then, draw a weather map to illustrate tomorrow's weather.

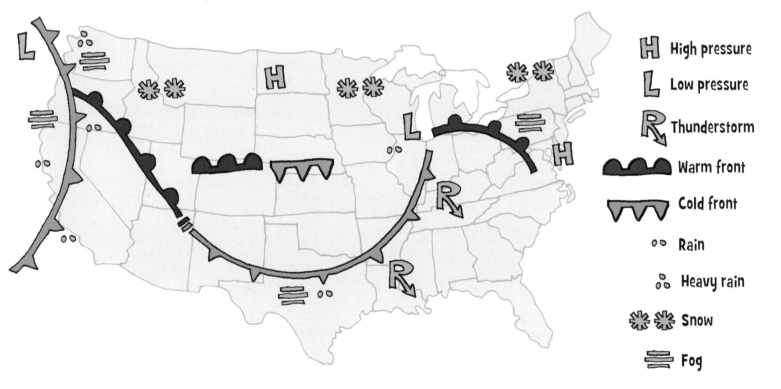

H	High pressure
L	Low pressure
R	Thunderstorm
⬤⬤⬤	Warm front
▽▽▽	Cold front
∘∘	Rain
⚬∘	Heavy rain
❋❋	Snow
☰	Fog

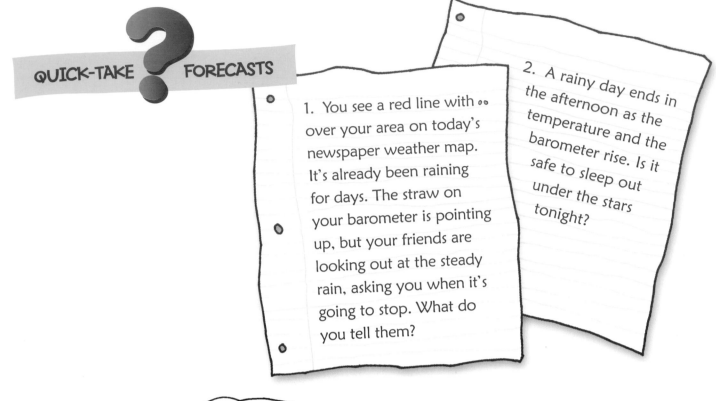

1. You see a red line with ●● over your area on today's newspaper weather map. It's already been raining for days. The straw on your barometer is pointing up, but your friends are looking out at the steady rain, asking you when it's going to stop. What do you tell them?

2. A rainy day ends in the afternoon as the temperature and the barometer rise. Is it safe to sleep out under the stars tonight?

Why are you pitching a tent? It stopped raining.

ANSWERS! 1. Let them know you'll all be able to play outside later in the day. When weather fronts are moving away, the air pressure rises. The rain should stop soon.

2. Better set up a tent. The pressure rising and the warmer air indicate a warm front. Remember that cold fronts often follow warm fronts, so a cold front is likely to arrive tonight or tomorrow. There's a good chance that you'll get wet as the cold front gets closer.

Weather—Always on the Move!

In North America, most weather is steered by the jet stream (see page 55), so it generally moves from west to east. This goes for fronts, pressure systems, and storms. Forecasters track these movements (and the speed at which they are moving) to predict the arrival of changing weather conditions.

HEY!

FORECASTER'S "GETTING IT RIGHT" RULES!

- A front, low, or storm to the northwest, west, or southwest may be heading toward you!

- A front, low, or storm to the southeast, east, or northeast is likely to be moving away from you.

HERE'S THE EXCEPTION: In the United States, on the Gulf Coast, in Florida, and along the southeastern coast to Virginia, hurricanes (see page 110) come from the east, the southeast, and the south.

FORECASTER'S "GETTING IT RIGHT" RULES!

- Storms often follow similar paths called *storm tracks.* Fair-weather systems also tend to follow similar paths.

- Storms get stronger wherever they pick up moisture: on the west coast of North America, in the Mississippi Valley north to the southern prairies of Canada and east to the Great Lakes, and along the East Coast.

- Storms lose their strength when they cross the coastal mountain ranges along the West Coast and as they head into the Rocky Mountains.

- Most storms travel at a constant speed.

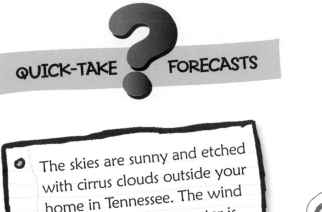

QUICK-TAKE ? FORECASTS

The skies are sunny and etched with cirrus clouds outside your home in Tennessee. The wind is light, and the barometer is not changing. But you've been watching a storm coming from the West Coast that brought rain to San Francisco yesterday. Today it has moved very quickly to western Oklahoma. Will this storm affect your family's plans to go for a hike tomorrow?

Harry! Come on! We have to be in Tennessee by tomorrow.

OKLAHOMA

ANSWER! Very likely yes. Even though the barometer is not changing, the cirrus clouds are the very first signs of a storm. Using a ruler or your finger, you can measure how far the storm has moved in the past 24 hours. Remember, storms typically move at a constant speed, so by tomorrow, that storm should be in Tennessee.

EL NIÑO AND LA NIÑA

El Niño is the name of a weather pattern that can really keep forecasters on their toes! Every three to seven years easterly winds along the west coast of South America become very light, so a current of warm tropical water moves farther east and south than usual. Water temperatures rise by a few degrees. Because this condition usually occurs around Christmas, the local residents began calling it El Niño, ("the boy child" in Spanish), referring to the Christ child.

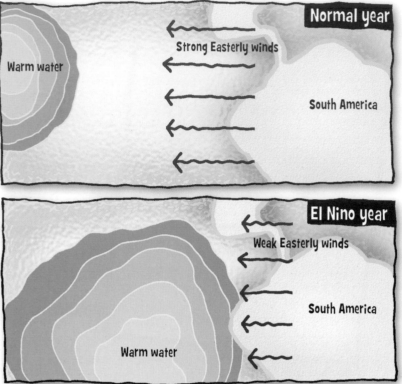

You wouldn't think that a slight warming of the ocean would be a big deal, but the results of El Niño can be catastrophic! Fish can't survive in the warmer water, which dramatically affects the region's fishing industry. El Niño can also cause unusually rainy summers in many parts of the world. In the United States, the Pacific Northwest will be warmer and drier during the winter, while the southeastern United States will be colder and stormier.

In years when these easterly winds are stronger than usual, a colder ocean current moves farther west than usual, creating a La Niña ("the girl child") weather pattern. Colder ocean temperatures during a La Niña year can cause winters to be warmer than normal in the southeastern United States and cooler than normal in the northwestern United States.

WEATHER RECORDS

In 1998, La Niña helped bring Mount Baker in Washington State the **world's record snowfall** for one season. From July 1998 to June 1999, *95 feet (29 m)* of snow fell! That same year, however, Florida, Louisiana, New Mexico, and Texas experienced the **driest period** ever recorded in those states.

What does your office look like?

I think many people are surprised that there isn't more equipment! I work with another meteorologist in a small office. There are two computer work stations and a weather desk with a bulletin board full of charts, formulas, and phone numbers that we use all the time. We have a small library of reference books, while the daily weather records of the past 100 years are in a handy file—we use them every day to create our forecasts.

I work in a museum, so my office has a glass wall on one side so visitors can look in while we work. People can watch us give live radio forecasts from the broadcasting booth too.

IS THE WEATHER CHANGING IN YOUR NEIGHBORHOOD?

What was the weather like in your town 10 years ago? How about 100 years ago? The daily weather records for your area are another tool you can use to fine-tune your forecasts, just as Mark does. Old newpapers and past editions of *The Old Farmer's Almanac* (at the local newspaper office or library) are great sources of climate information.

For more detailed information about climate records in the United States, contact your state climatologist through the American Association of State Climatologists, Illinois State Water Survey, 2204 Griffith Dr., Champaign, IL 61820-7495.

In Canada, contact the Climate Data Centre at the Meteorological Service of Canada, Inquiry Center, 351 St. Joseph Boulevard, Hull, Quebec, K1A 0H3.

Try It: Research past dates and temperatures for your area and record them in your Weather Log. Do they match the weather memories you recorded (see page 105)? Compare them with this year's weather. Do you see a trend?

Take a Survey

How much are weather and climate a matter of fact and how much are they perception (what people remember about them)? Ask a group of people to describe the climate where you live (don't forget to include your own impressions). Then ask each person to describe the weather over the past season or two ("We had a dry summer and it was very hot, but the fall was cold and dreary."). See how many people agree on recent weather. Then check your own Weather Log or with a local weather forecaster. Are the people you surveyed mostly correct or do memory and personal experience change impressions?

THE TELL-TALE TREE

Here's another way to learn about the weather of the past: look inside a tree and examine its growth rings! In years when the weather was warm and moist and the tree could grow easily, the growth rings are wide. Where rings are narrow, it was dry or cold (or both), and the tree couldn't grow as much.

Climate scientists in the southwestern United States have used the Douglas fir and the bristlecone pine to accurately date events and climatic conditions of the past 3,000 to 4,000 years. There is even evidence of volcanic eruptions in these trees' growth rings! (The smoke and ash from the volcanoes blocked sunlight, causing cooler temperatures.)

Try It: Find a tree stump in your neighborhood. Trace the rings onto a sheet of thin paper. Each ring shows a year in the life of the tree, with the center ring being the oldest. How old was the tree when it first experienced a period of dry or cold weather? Any volcanoes in its past? Now, check the tree's "recorded" history against weather records—do they agree?

WEATHER WORDS

Weather satellites are like mini-spaceships carrying meteorological instruments. They take measurements of the clouds in the upper atmosphere and transmit information and pictures of the weather back to earth from outer space so computers can analyze them. This view from above has given meteorologists a whole new understanding of weather patterns!

The weather satellite on the top of this rocket will be released in space, where it will orbit the earth.

ASK MARK!

Can you tell me about a time when you really got it wrong?

When I began forecasting almost 20 years ago, I didn't have the computers and satellite information available today. One morning during my first summer of forecasting, I was on the radio talking about what a beautiful morning it was—going on about the blue skies and the birds singing. Just after I finished my forecast, I got a phone call from a listener 150 miles (241 km) away who thought I was crazy! He was having a terrible thunderstorm with hail and wild winds—definitely not a "beautiful" morning!

There is an old superstition that if the brown bands on **woolly bear caterpillars** are wide, winter will be mild, but if the black bands are wide, winter will be harsh. When scientists at the American Museum of Natural History studied this belief, however, they didn't find any connection between the stripes and the weather. It's still fun to hunt for those fuzzy little caterpillars, though, isn't it?

For added fun, jot down in your log what you observe about their stripes. Then, make your winter forecast and see how much the woolly bears told you.

I'll trade you this leaf for a forecast...

ASK MARK!

I'd like to see some meteorologists in action! Where do I go?

There are lots of places! Ask a grownup to call the nearest U. S. National Weather Service office (check the United States Government listings in the white pages under Commerce Department) to arrange a convenient time to visit. To visit a local office of the Meteorological Service of Canada, check the blue pages listings for NAV CANADA. You can also visit a local TV station or university weather station. Take notes in your Weather Log, or bring along a tape recorder.

Here are some of the things the kids who visit me at work like to do:

- watch me use weather instruments and record data, and ask me questions about how the equipment works

- see where I make my forecasts (and observe me on air giving one, if possible!)

- make a forecast before they arrive—and then compare it to my forecast!

When ditch and pond affect the nose, look out for rain and stormy blows.

Before the earliest weather tools were invented, people relied on their **five senses** to tell them what the weather would be. Of course, they could spot dark clouds and hear thunder, but could they smell when a storm was coming? Yes! Not only will ditches and ponds smell right before rain—manure will stink more than usual, and flowers will smell even sweeter! Our sense of smell is stronger when the air is moist, so we are more likely to detect the odors given off by soil and plants.

Try It: When your weather observations and equipment indicate a storm is headed your way, go outside and take a big whiff. If it's not already raining, can you smell—I mean tell—the storm is coming?

BE A
METEOROLOGIST

LOW-TECH WEATHER TRACKING

Meteorologists certainly need to use high-tech tools to keep up with modern-day weather tracking. But that doesn't mean they forget to use their own five senses and simple observation skills. You might be surprised at how much you can forecast just by looking out the window or walking around outside.

What predictions can **you** make based on these simple observations?

1. **Flags:** Are they hanging from the flag poles or flapping wildly? In what direction are they pointing?

2. **Trees and branches:** Are they still, swaying slowly, or bending way over?

3. **Grass:** Is it dry or damp?

4. **Clothes on the clothesline:** Are they hanging straight down or waving? After a day, do they still feel damp?

5. **Air:** What does it feel like on your skin? What does it smell like?

6. **Birds:** How active are they? Are they sitting "poofed up" on the branches?

7. **Pets:** Does your cat or dog want to go outside?

ANSWERS!

1. Flags will indicate wind speed and direction.

2. Trees and branches will indicate wind speed.

3. Remember "Dew on the grass" (see page 69).

4. Flapping clothes will indicate wind speed. If clothes dry quickly, the air is dry. Damp clothes signal humid weather.

5. A lot of water vapor in the air can make you feel "sticky" (and don't forget your own hair!). Also, remember "When ditch and pond affect the nose" (see page 130).

6. Birds often feed vigorously before a storm. When the weather is very cold, they puff out their feathers to create an insulating layer of air under them.

7. Animals often act "nervous" and change their behaviors before a storm.

With all this computerized satellite data, why does it seem that the weather forecast is sometimes, well, wrong?

Weather forecasts are only as good as the information forecasters start with and our understanding of how the weather works. Both of those things are getting better all the time. There are still times, however, when a storm is stronger than our data indicates, so forecasters start out with inaccurate information. And we don't know everything there is to know about the weather, so our forecasts are not perfect!

Clouds are high-flying...

Here are some weather funnies that kids wrote!

- Water vapor gets together in a cloud. When it is big enough to be called a drop, it does.

- Humidity is when you look for air and find water.

- Rain is saved up in cloud banks.

- The wind is like the air, only pushier.

- A blizzard is when it snows sideways.

Try writing your own weather one-liners! Post a different one each week and you'll have your family laughing up a storm, while you teach them a thing or two about the weather.

What dream invention would make your job easier?

A faster computer.

Sound simple? Consider that the world's fastest computers are already used for forecasting the weather, and the forecast still takes over three hours to calculate!

If I had a faster computer, I could feed the newest information right in and see how it affected the predictions in an instant. Then I could fine-tune my predictions and say, for example, "If the temperature is more than 85°F (29°C) today, watch out for thunderstorms. But if the temperature is less than 85°F (29°C), it won't rain."

Invent a Weather Maker

Draw a diagram of your own future weather invention. How will your invention help people? How will it affect other animals? Trees? Oceans? Think about your invention carefully so you don't end up changing the weather in ways you didn't intend.

Maybe you will be the one to invent a machine that will blow big storms out into space, or will make air pressure rise, so the sun will always shine down on our summer barbecues!

RELATIVE HUMIDITY IN °CELSIUS

Where the columns are blank, the relative humidity is zero (or very close). When you have a very large difference between the dry- and wet-bulb temperatures, the relative humidity is so small that you can't measure it (less than one percent).

Difference between dry- and wet-bulb Temperatures

°C	1	2	3	4	5	6	7	8	9	10
4	85	70	56	42	27	14				
5	85	71	58	44	31	18	5			
6	86	72	59	46	35	22	10			
7	86	73	60	48	37	25	14	3		
8	87	74	62	51	39	28	17	6		
9	87	75	63	53	41	31	20	10	3	
10	88	77	66	55	44	34	24	15	6	
11	89	78	67	56	46	36	27	18	9	
12	89	78	68	58	48	39	29	21	12	
13	89	79	69	59	50	41	32	22	15	7
14	90	79	70	60	51	42	34	26	18	10
15	90	80	71	61	53	44	36	27	20	13
16	90	81	71	63	54	46	38	30	23	15
17	90	81	72	64	55	47	40	32	25	18
18	91	82	73	65	57	49	41	34	27	20
19	91	82	74	65	58	50	43	36	29	22
20	91	83	74	67	59	53	46	39	32	26
21	91	83	75	67	60	53	46	39	32	26
22	92	83	76	68	61	54	47	40	34	28
23	92	84	76	69	62	56	49	43	37	31
24	92	84	77	69	62	56	49	43	37	31
25	92	84	77	70	63	57	50	44	39	33
26	92	85	77	70	64	57	51	45	39	34
27	92	85	77	70	64	58	52	46	40	35
28	93	86	78	71	65	59	53	47	42	36
29	93	86	78	71	65	60	54	48	43	38
30	93	86	79	72	66	61	55	49	44	39
31	93	86	79	72	67	61	55	50	45	40
32	93	86	80	73	68	62	56	51	46	41

Dry-bulb Temperature

RELATIVE HUMIDITY IN °FAHRENHEIT

If your dry-bulb temperature falls between the two numbers in the left-hand column, you'll have to estimate the relative humidity. For example, a dry-bulb temperature of 47° (halfway between 46° and 48°) with a dry-wet difference of 15° will fall about halfway between 3 and 7, or 5%.

Difference between dry- and wet-bulb Temperatures

°F	1	2	3	4	5	6	7	8	9	10	11	12	13	14	15	16	17	18	19	20
40	92	84	76	68	60	53	45	38	30	22	16	8	1							
42	92	84	77	69	62	55	48	40	34	27	20	13	6							
44	92	85	78	72	63	57	50	43	27	30	24	17	11	5						
46	93	85	79	72	65	58	52	46	39	33	27	21	15	9	3					
48	93	86	79	73	66	60	53	48	42	36	30	24	19	13	7	2				
50	93	87	80	74	67	61	55	50	44	38	33	27	22	16	11	6	1			
52	94	87	81	75	69	63	57	51	46	40	35	30	24	20	15	10	5			
54	94	88	82	76	70	64	59	53	48	43	38	33	28	23	18	13	8	4		
56	94	89	82	77	17	65	60	55	50	44	40	35	30	25	21	16	12	8	3	
58	94	89	83	78	72	67	61	56	51	46	42	37	33	28	24	19	15	11	7	2
60	94	89	84	78	73	68	63	58	53	48	44	39	34	30	26	22	18	14	10	6
62	95	89	84	79	74	69	64	59	54	50	45	41	37	32	28	24	20	16	13	9
64	95	90	85	79	74	70	65	60	56	51	47	43	38	34	30	27	23	19	15	12
66	95	90	85	80	75	71	66	61	57	53	49	45	40	35	32	29	25	22	18	14
68	95	90	85	81	76	71	67	63	58	54	50	46	42	38	34	31	27	24	20	17
70	95	90	86	81	77	72	68	64	60	55	52	48	44	40	36	33	29	26	23	19
72	95	91	86	82	77	73	69	65	61	57	53	49	45	42	38	35	31	28	24	23
74	95	91	86	82	78	74	70	65	62	58	54	50	47	43	40	36	33	30	26	23
76	95	91	87	83	78	74	70	66	63	59	55	52	48	45	41	38	35	31	28	25
78	96	91	87	83	79	75	71	67	63	60	56	53	49	46	43	39	37	33	30	27
80	96	92	87	83	79	75	72	68	64	61	57	54	51	47	44	41	38	35	32	29
82	96	92	88	84	80	76	72	69	65	62	58	55	52	48	45	42	39	36	33	31
84	96	92	88	84	80	77	73	69	66	63	59	56	53	49	46	44	41	38	35	32
86	96	92	88	84	88	77	73	70	67	63	60	57	54	51	48	45	42	39	36	34
88	96	92	88	85	81	77	74	71	67	64	61	58	55	52	49	46	43	40	38	35
90	96	93	88	85	81	78	75	71	68	65	62	59	56	53	50	47	44	41	39	36

Dry-bulb Temperature

THE WEATHERMAN SONG

Music and Lyrics by Mark Breen

Chorus:

1: WHO'D HAVE EV - ER THOUGHT I'D WRITE A SONG A - BOUT THE WEA - THER - MAN?
3 & 5: HERE IS MY SONG, DED - I - CA - TED TO THE WEA - THER - MAN,

1, 3, 5: MOD - ERN FOLK-DAY HE - RO, WHO IS TRYIN' TO HELP US UN - DER - STAND;

1 & 5: WEA - THER IS - N'T GOOD OR BAD, AND YOU CAN REST AS - SURED, THE
3: WEA - THER IS - N'T GOOD OR BAD, IT IS - N'T RIGHT OR WRONG, AND

1 & 5: ON - LY THING HE'S SURE OF IS WE'RE BOUND TO HAVE SOME MORE ———— !
3: IF YOU'LL JUST AC - CEPT IT, WELL, I THINK WE'LL GET A - LONG ———— !

Verse ①②

2: THINK A - BOUT YOUR WEA - THER - MAN IN RAD - I - O OR T - V LAND,
4: WEA - THER-MEN DON'T MAKE THE WEA - THER, THEY DON'T BLOW —— THE SNOW,

2: TRYIN' NOT TO LOSE YOU WITH THOSE TERMS THAT CAN CON - FUSE YOU ——! HE
4: THEY DON'T ASK THE CLOUDS TO COME IN, OR THE SUN TO GO ——, SO

2: TALKS A - BOUT HIS HIGHS AND LOWS, BUT THEY DON'T HOLD A FEA - THER TO
4: IF YOU HEAR THE FORECAST AND IT'S CALL - ING FOR RAIN ——.

2: LOOK - ING OUT THE WIN - DOW IF YOU WANT TO KNOW THE WEA - THER !

4: PLEASE BE - LIEVE THE WEA - THER - MAN, HE CAN'T BE WRONG A - GAIN !

RESOURCES

Books

Eyewitness Explorers: Weather.
John Farndon and John Bendall-Brunello.
Dorling Kindersley, Inc., 1998

It's Raining Cats and Dogs—All Kinds of Weather, and Why We Have It. *Franklyn M. Branley.*
Houghton Mifflin Co., 1987

National Audubon Society First Field Guide: Weather.
Jonathan D.W. Kahl. Scholastic, 1998

Peterson First Guide to Clouds and Weather. *John Day, Vincent J. Schaefer, and Roger Tory Peterson.*
Houghton Mifflin Co., 1998

Weather. *Paul Lehr, Will Burnett and Herbert Spenser Zim.* Golden Press, 1987

The Weather Book. *Jack Williams.*
Random House, Inc., 1997

Weather Experiments.
Vera R. Webster. Children's Press, 1989

Weather Wisdom—Facts and Folklore of Weather Forecasting.
Albert Lee. Congdon & Weed, Inc., 1990

Weather Organizations

National Oceanic and Atmospheric Administration, Silver Spring, MD
www.noaa.gov
Broadcasts continuous weather information 24 hours a day and issues weather warnings via the more than 300 NOAA Weather Radio Stations.

U.S. National Weather Service, Silver Spring, MD
www.nws.noaa.gov
Part of the NOAA, the NWS makes about two million forecasts a year. It also sends out storm and flood warnings and nearly 750,000 forecasts for aircraft.

National Climatic Data Center, Asheville, NC
www.ncdc.noaa.gov
World's largest archive of weather data: climate records, weather extremes, and storm data.

National Hurricane Center, Miami, FL
www.nhc.noaa.gov
Uses satellites, radar, airplanes, and weather balloons to predict the force and path of hurricanes.

National Severe Storms Laboratory, Norman, OK
www.nssl.noaa.gov
Located in the heart of Tornado Alley, the National Weather Service coordinates this joint civilian-military effort to track and study tornadoes and other severe storms.

The Meteorological Service of Canada, "Weather Office"
http://www.weatheroffice.gc.ca
Issues more than one million public, marine, and aviation forecasts a year. Broadcasts severe weather warnings via Canada's Weatheradio.

Weather on The Web

Eye on the Sky
http://eotsweb.org
Read Mark's detailed forecasts and his weather blog. Includes a glossary of weather-related terminology.

El Niño Theme Page
www.pmel.noaa.gov
Includes 3-D animations of El Niño and La Niña and Frequently Asked Questions.

The Old Farmer's Almanac
www.almanac.com
Find out what happened "today in weather history." Seven-day and long-range forecasts are also available.

The Hurricane Hunters
www.hurricanehunters.com
Take a "Cyberflight" along with the Hurricane Hunters right through a hurricane! The site includes photos, animated radar images, and Frequently Asked Questions.

Dan's Wild, Wild Weather Page
http://www.wildwildweather.com
Includes games and puzzles, weather quizzes, and weather information on more than two hundred locations around the world.

Sky Diary: Storm Chasing, Photography & Rainy-Day Tales
http://www.skydiary.com
Includes amazing photos of weather—from lightning to tornadoes to rainbows, along with lots of information on tracking storms.

USA Today
www.usatoday.com/weather
Here you can find rain maps, five-day forecasts, and information on weather-tracking instruments. Extensive list of topics.

The Weather Channel
www.weather.com
The website for cable TV's The Weather Channel. Radar and satellite maps as well as ten-day forecasts.

"The Weather Dude"
www.wxdude.com
Hosted by Nick Walker of The Weather Channel, this site has forecasts, maps, songs, quizzes, maps, and other materials.

Web Weather for Kids
http://eo.ucar.edu/webweather
Learn even more about weather through the glossary and Weather Ingredients page, do fun weather-related activities and experiments, and play games.

Index

More Good Books from Williamson Books

Williamson Books are available from your bookseller or directly from Ideals Publications.
Please see last page for ordering information or to visit our website.

Parent's Guide Children's Media Award
Alphabet Art
With A to Z Animal Art
& Fingerplays
BY JUDY PRESS

Around-the-World Art & Activities
Visiting the 7 Continents
through Craft Fun
BY JUDY PRESS

Awesome Ocean Science
Investigating the Secrets of the
Underwater World
BY CINDY A. LITTLEFIELD

Bridges!
Amazing Structures to Design,
Build & Test
BY CAROL A. JOHMANN AND
ELIZABETH J. RIETH

China
Over 40 Activities to Experience
China—Past and Present
BY DEBBI MICHIKO FLORENCE

Crafts Across America
More than 40 Crafts that Immigrated
to America
BY CINDY A. LITTLEFIELD

Eco Art!
Earth-Friendly Art & Craft Experiences
for 3- to 9-year-olds
BY LAURIE CARLSON

Fizz, Bubble & Flash!
Element Explorations & Atom
Adventures for Hands-On Science Fun!
BY ANITA BRANDOLINI, PH.D.

Parents' Choice Gold Award
Fun with My 5 Senses
Activities to Build Learning Readiness
BY SARAH. A. WILLIAMSON

Geology Rocks!
50 Hands-On Activities to
Explore the Earth
BY CINDY BLOBAUM

Gizmos & Gadgets
Creating Science Contraptions
That Work (& Knowing Why)
BY JILL FRANKEL HAUSER

Going West!
Journey on a Wagon Train to Settle a
Frontier Town
BY CAROL A. JOHMANN AND
ELIZABETH J. RIETH

Great Games!
Old & New, Indoor/Outdoor, Board,
Card, Ball & Word
BY SAM TAGGAR

Japan
Over 40 Activities to Experience
Japan—Past and Present
BY DEBBI MICHIKO FLORENCE

Keeping Our Earth Green
Over 100 Hands-On Ways to Help
Save the Earth
BY NANCY F. CASTALDO

Kids Cook!
Fabulous Food for
the Whole Family
BY SARAH WILLIAMSON &
ZACHARY WILLIAMSON

Kids' Easy-to-Create Wildlife Habitats
for Small Spaces in City, Suburb,
and Countryside
BY EMILY STETSON

The Kid's Guide to Becoming the Best You Can Be!
Developing 5 traits you need to
achieve your personal best
BY JILL FRANKEL HAUSER

The Kids' Multicultural Art Book
Art & Craft Experiences
from Around the World
BY ALEXANDRA MICHAELS

Parents' Choice Approved
Skipping Stones Multicultural
Honor Award
Benjamin Franklin Best
Multicultural Book Award
The Kids' Multicultural Cookbook
Food & Fun Around the World
BY DEANNA F. COOK

Leap Into Space
Exploring the Universe and Your Place
in It
BY NANCY F. CASTALDO

Parent's Guide Classic Award
LifeWorks Magazine Real Life Award
The Little Hands Art Book
Exploring Arts & Crafts
with 2- to 6-year-olds
BY JUDY PRESS

The Little Hands Big Fun Craft Book
Creative Fun for 2- to 6-Year Olds
BY JUDY PRESS

Little Hands Celebrate America
Learning about the U.S.A.
through Crafts & Activities
BY JILL FRANKEL HAUSER

Parents' Choice Recommended
Making Amazing Art!
40 Activities Using the
7 Elements of Art Design
BY SANDI HENRY

American Bookseller Pick of the Lists
Math Play!
80 Ways to Count & Learn
BY DIANE MCGOWAN & MARK SCHROOTEN

Monarch Magic!
Butterfly Activities &
Nature Discoveries
BY LYNN M. ROSENBLATT

Science Play!
Beginning Discoveries
for 2- to 6-Year-Olds
BY JILL FRANKEL HAUSER

Skyscrapers!
Super Structures to Design & Build
BY CAROL A. JOHMANN

Super Science Concoctions
50 Mysterious Mixtures for
Fabulous Fun
BY JILL FRANKEL HAUSER

Using Color in Your Art!
Choosing Colors for
Impact & Pizzazz
BY SANDI HENRY

Little Hands® and *Kids Can!*® are registered
trademarks of Ideals Publications.

Visit Our Website!

To see what's new with Williamson Books and Ideals Publications and learn more about specific titles, visit our website at: www.idealsbooks.com

To Order Books:

You'll find Williamson Books at your favorite bookstore, or you can order directly from Ideals Publications. We accept Visa and MasterCard (please include the number and expiration date).

Order on our secure website: www.idealsbooks.com

Toll-free phone orders with credit cards: 1-800-586-2572

Toll-free fax orders: 1-888-815-2759

Or send a check with your order to:
Ideals Publications
Williamson Books Orders
2630 Elm Hill Pike, Suite 100
Nashville, Tennessee 37214

Catalog request: web, mail, or phone

Please add **$4.00** for postage for one book plus **$1.00** for each additional book. Satisfaction is guaranteed or full refund without questions or quibbles.